The Mordecai Mantle

The Mordecai Mantle

Nations Hanging in the Balance, Hamans Hanging on Their Gallows

LORI PERZ

2nd Edition

Copyright © 2021 Lori Perz

All rights reserved.

No part of this publication may be reproduced, distributed, or transmitted in any form or by any means, including photocopying, recording, or other electronic or mechanical methods, without the prior written permission of the author, except in the case of brief quotations embodied in critical reviews and certain other noncommercial uses permitted by copyright law. For permission requests, send an email to the author, addressed to: ariseandshine444@protonmail.com.

Cover design: Haley Perz

eBook ISBN: 978-1-7347991-2-5
Paperback ISBN: 978-1-7347991-1-8

Printed in the United States of America

Scripture (unless otherwise noted) taken from the New King James Version®. Copyright © 1982 by Thomas Nelson. Used by permission.

Scripture quotations marked TPT are from The Passion Translation®. Copyright © 2017, 2018 by Passion & Fire Ministries, Inc. Used by permission. All rights reserved. ThePassionTranslation.com.

DEDICATION

To Jason, my super hero.

THE MORDECAI MANTLE

CONTENTS

1	For Such a Time as This	1
2	An Ancient Foe	9
3	Trauma to Triumph	15
4	New Apostolic Era	25
5	The Warrior and the Hidden Star	31
6	Write a New Decree	37
7	Justice at Just the Right Time	45
8	Transfigure and Radiate	51
9	Turning the Tables	59
	Acknowledgements	67
	About the Author	71

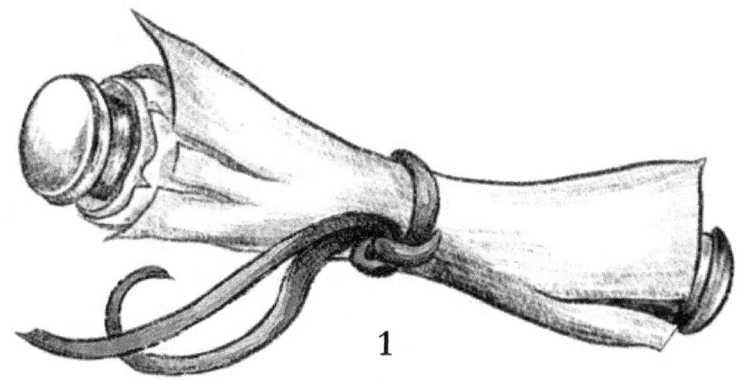

1

FOR SUCH A TIME AS THIS

"For such a time as this". This is truly an iconic phrase, taken directly from the Book of Esther in the Bible (Esther 4:14). It is a profound destiny statement, spoken in a moment of great crisis in a young queen's life--and in her nation.

If you're not familiar with the Book of Esther, it will be unpacked throughout this book. But, here is a brief summary of this remarkable account to provide a backdrop: a Persian (modern-day Iran) king named Ahaseurus is greatly displeased with his queen, so he calls for a search among the maidens in his kingdom for a new queen. Part of his kingdom includes the Jewish people, who were taken into exile there.

Esther is a young woman and orphan, brought into the care of her cousin Mordecai who adopted her. She is chosen to be one of the maidens taken back to the king's palace and made part of his harem. She ends up pleasing the king and selected to be his new queen.

Mordecai is also a part of the king's government, as he serves as an official. Another official to the king, Haman, is enraged that Mordecai won't bow down to him. Haman hatches a plan to trick the king into writing a decree to not only kill Mordecai but every Jewish person. After hearing this horrific news, Esther calls a three-day fast for all of her people.

Esther has to decide if she will risk her life to go before the king unannounced and bravely decides to do so. Her strategy involves hosting two banquets, back to back, that the king and Haman are invited to. At the second banquet, she reveals her identity as a Jew and pulls back the curtains on Haman's evil schemes. The king is outraged and ends up having Haman hung on the very gallows that had been built for Mordecai.

In the end, both Mordecai and Esther are promoted and given great favor. They write a new decree to override the king's initial one, and the Jewish people are given the right to bear arms and rise up and fight. The tables are turned and they soundly conquer their enemy! The holiday of Purim is then instituted as a time to annually remember and celebrate this stunning victory over their enemies!

In context of this "against all odds" turnaround story, consider that "for such as time as this" also resounds a kairos, opportune moment from God. It's when eternity intersects time and what is written in a scroll in heaven is ripe to burst forth. It's a moment of Holy Spirit hovering, waiting for a "yes" so that what is written can manifest into the "now" time. It's a birthing from heaven to earth.

The Mordecai Mantle will take a closer look at the distinguished man behind this epic phrase. You could also say the "man behind the queen". He stepped into such a destiny moment and issued a challenge to distraught Queen Esther to rise up in her destiny as well. He punctuated his appeal with this clincher: "for such a time is this". It was directed to her in a do-or-die moment of her life and Mordecai's life--and the life of the Jewish people.

Esther is, in many ways, the star of the Book of Esther. Even her name means "star". However, Mordecai is just as stellar as this historic queen. He was an anointed leader whom God appointed, right on time, to not only be written in the annals of history but to be recorded in the canon of Scripture, the Word of God! God used him to literally preserve a nation.

Listen to these weighty words from Mordecai, pointed straight at the heart of Esther: "For if you remain silent at this time, relief and deliverance for the Jews will arise from another place, but you and your father's family will perish. And who knows but that you have come to royal position for such a time as this?" (Esther 4:14).

Just as in the days of Mordecai approximately 2,500 years ago, there is now an existential crisis that America faces. The enemy of this nation is stopping at nothing to destroy it and its people. He knows that America's destiny as a "city on a hill" profoundly impacts not just this nation but the nations of the earth. Right now, many nations are also hanging in the balance. But God! He is releasing unprecedented justice and turning the tables in extraordinary ways—just like He did in the national crisis that Mordecai, Esther and the Jewish people faced.

Suddenly Turnaround and Promotion

As noted, the Book of Esther recounts one of the most remarkable turnarounds in history. In a stunning turn of events orchestrated by God, the evil enemy of the Jewish people, Haman, literally hung on the very gallows he built to murder Mordecai. Queen Esther and Mordecai arose together to see their lives spared and their people not only rescued but advanced in their destiny. These two heroic figures also experienced incredible "suddenly" promotion and favor.

Once again, we are in similar circumstances in America right now. God has summoned His sons and daughters, of each generation, to not only rise up bravely as Esthers but to receive the Mordecai "mantle" that helps to nurture, equip, watch over and prepare the Esthers. The Esthers and Mordecais of the land are aligning together in the Spirit of God--to overcome the enemy, preserve an entire nation and call it forth in its God-given destiny.

Allow this journey in *The Mordecai Mantle* to inspire and encourage you to know Father God in a deeper way, to know your identity more clearly and to courageously play your part in this end of days drama. What's unfolding is one of the greatest triumphs over the enemy that history has witnessed. The global harvest of a billion-plus souls is here and you have a key note to sound in the orchestra! Arise and shine for the glory of the Lord now rises upon you (Isaiah 60:1-2). Our Bridegroom King is coming!

Life or Death

Let's begin by taking a closer look at the scenario that "for such a time as this" was spoken into. In Esther chapter 4, we learn that the Persian King Ahaseurus had just issued a decree to kill all of the Jewish people, essentially tricked by wicked Haman, one of his top officials and advisors. "When Mordecai learned all that had happened, he tore his clothes and put on sackcloth and ashes, and went out into the midst of the city. He cried out with a loud and bitter cry. He went as far as the front of the king's gate, for no one might enter the king's gate clothed with sackcloth. And in every province where the king's command and decree arrived, there was great mourning among the Jews, with fasting, weeping, and wailing; and many lay in sackcloth and ashes" (Esther 4:1-3).

Queen Esther heard the distressing news through her maids and the king's eunuchs. "Esther spoke to Hathach, and gave him a command for Mordecai: 'All the king's servants and the people of the king's provinces know that any man or woman who goes into the inner court to the king, who has not been called, he has but one law: put all to death, except the one to whom the king holds out the golden scepter, that he may live. Yet I myself have not been called to go in to the king these thirty days.' So they told Mordecai Esther's words" (Esther 4:10-11). It is then that Mordecai's "for such a time as this" reply is given like a weighty summons to the queen who literally faces death if she approaches the king in an improper manner. Without the king's approval through granting her his golden scepter, she would be killed.

Turning of the Tables

Trying to comprehend the weight of what Esther, and Mordecai, faced in that moment is impossible for most of us who have never faced such a dire situation. And yet, when we look at what is at stake in America right now (and many nations), we can clearly see it is a life-or-death kind of reality. This is why the subtitle of this book is "Nations Hanging in the Balance, Hamans Hanging on Their Gallows".

The Word of God says: "For we do not wrestle against flesh and blood, but against principalities, against powers, against the rulers of the darkness of this age, against spiritual hosts of wickedness in the heavenly places" (Ephesians 6:12). To state it plainly, there are ancient, high-level demonic forces and thrones, ultimately connected to the fallen sons of God, that have been systematically operating through human agents. These ancient powers have modern faces, and many of these evil agents have been systematically plotting the death of America and the destruction of its destiny. For decades and even centuries! This is not an exaggeration.

But God! Just as He did in Mordecai's day, God has a stunning plan to turn the tables on the enemy! Instead of two people, He is now calling forth an army of Mordecais (and Esthers) to come forth as deliverers.

Mordecai seized the moment in this extreme crisis his people faced. In the wisdom of God, he called a young-girl-turned-queen to come up higher. He appealed to her human spirit, not only her soul. Through a messenger, he urged her to not only be concerned with her own preservation, but to look beyond to see the panoramic destiny of her entire people. Even future generations were at stake. Esther received his challenge and she took courageous action, literally risking her own life to save her people.

God worked through her sacrifice, as well as Mordecai's bravery, and brought a stunning turn of events to not only rescue the Jewish people but to bring enlargement to them. *This is what the feast of Purim in the Book of Esther is about: a nation facing genocide and God's miraculous turning of the tables through two of His chosen vessels.*

What joy comes from this dimension of triumph over the enemy! Jewish and Christian people all over the world continue to celebrate Purim every year in the Hebraic month of Adar. It's a time to remember this epic victory (and the defeat of evil Haman) and a feast of great merriment and joy!

Consider that Purim is more than a time to look back at a stunning victory and celebrate. This feast can actually inspire us to step into this dimension of triumph and overcoming--and joy--in our own lives *now*! It's a "Purim paradigm" that we can literally experience any day of the year! This is because of the victory that already was secured by Jesus' death on the cross and His resurrection power. This power dwells within His sons and daughters by the Spirit of God, Holy Spirit.

"God always makes his grace visible in Christ, who includes us as partners of his endless triumph. Through our yielded lives he spreads the fragrance of the knowledge of God everywhere we go" (2 Corinthians 2:14 TPT). Did you catch that phrase, "endless triumph"? Triumph means not just winning the battle, but conquest—dominating the enemy! That's our inheritance!

Miraculous Purim Turnaround

Esther could not have risen up to take such bold, decisive action if it had not been for Mordecai's faithful training, modeling, nurturing, and coaching as her father—and most certainly his watchful intercession for her. They were interdependent with each other and God designed it that way.

There is an "army" of Mordecais that God is calling to watchfully intercede and support Esthers in this time of history. They are arising together to see the miraculous turnaround of a nation and the Haman spirit hang on its gallows!

Purim is a time gate of triumph--a key gate for turnaround. God is using what the enemy intends for harm to bring good--to bring awakening to hearts and set the stage for greater global harvest! Salvation, healing and deliverance breaking out to the multitudes!

This is His covenantal mercy, His chesed! "Oh, give thanks to the LORD, for He is good! For His mercy [chesed] endures forever" (Psalm 107:1). We give thanks to you, Father God, for your unfailing kindness and mercy to us—by covenant.

National Turnaround: Nehemiah and Esther Parallels

As we look at both the Book of Esther and the Book of Nehemiah, *there are stunning parallels between the national turnarounds in both of these accounts.* Mordecai, Esther and Nehemiah displayed character traits and took action that have incredible similarity. Even more, there is powerful application for us and the times we are living in right now:

1. In both accounts, a nation was in crisis. In Esther and Mordecai's day, the Jewish people were literally facing a holocaust. In Nehemiah's time, the "wall of Jerusalem was broken down and its gates were on fire" (Nehemiah 1:3).
2. Both Esther and Nehemiah responded to this crisis with a spiritual solution: repentance, fasting and prayer.
3. We see great favor given to Mordecai, as he received the king's royal robe, royal horse and signet ring (authority of the king). Incredible favor from God was also upon Esther, who "won the favor of

everyone who saw her" (Esther 2:15). As for Nehemiah, he also "found favor in [the king's] sight" (Nehemiah 2:5).
4. Mordecai, Esther and Nehemiah were promoted and positioned by God into high-ranking positions in a foreign government in order to preserve and rebuild the nation.
5. A humble, but bold approach to the king with a weighty request is found in both the Book of Esther and the Book of Nehemiah. Great discretion was also employed.
6. All three of these leaders displayed a sacrificial willingness to risk their lives. Esther could have been killed for approaching the king unannounced and Nehemiah risked execution by displeasing the king with his sorrowful countenance.
7. The king essentially asked both Esther and Nehemiah, "What do you want me to do?" (Nehemiah 2:4; Esther 5:3). Both of them not only made one request, but several appeals to the king--those requests were granted.
8. Covert intel for key assignments was given from Mordecai to Esther. Nehemiah received this intel through his secret nocturnal assignment to survey the gates of Jerusalem (Nehemiah 2:11-16).
9. Because of the spiritual leadership and bold action of Nehemiah, Mordecai and Esther, their people were emboldened, inspired and mobilized to also rise up in renewed courage to do their part to take back the land.
10. In the storylines of Mordecai, Esther and Nehemiah, miraculous turnaround took place and the entire nation was not only preserved but advanced!

Full Circle of Freedom

In the second chapter of Nehemiah it states, "In the month of Nisan..." (Nehemiah 2:1). Nehemiah approaches the king with his requests to rebuild the wall of Jerusalem, and the Scripture states: "Then the king, with the queen sitting beside him..." (Nehemiah 2:6). *Although Bible scholars differ on who this king and queen were, some believe that they were King Ahaseurus and Queen Esther!* If this is accurate, this is astonishing!

Mordecai raised up Esther as her father and then coached her in times of great crisis as a queen. The two of them together preserved the entire Jewish race. Years after the turning of the tables with the "new decree" that they wrote together, she is sitting as queen next to King Ahaseurus. And now, instead of her being the one to make a bold appeal, she is seeing a fellow Jew, Nehemiah, coming before her and her king to also risk his life in order to preserve the nation. What a remarkable full circle.

God is a multigenerational God. He moved mightily through Mordecai and Esther to save the nation. This freedom torch was then passed to Nehemiah and his people, to continue the work that God wanted completed in rebuilding the temple. *This was much more than restoring the physical walls and gates, it was ultimately about the spiritual restoration that God wanted to bring to His people.* Ezra the scribe joined Nehemiah in being very instrumental for this call from God to bring reformation.

And now, that freedom torch for reformation has been passed to you and me.

Grab Ahold of the Freedom Torch and Arise!

It's NOW time for us to receive this freedom torch from our spiritual ancestors of Mordecai and Nehemiah, Ezra and Daniel and others…to fully possess the kingdom (Daniel 7:22). We are contending for not only the physical restoration of our nation, but the spiritual restoration that God has promised in this Third Great Awakening. We have a key part to play, just like Mordecai, Esther and Nehemiah did!

Arise in strength and power and shine (Isaiah 60:1-2), like the royal son or daughter you are called to be. You have been prepared. You have been positioned and promoted for such a time as this (Esther 4:14). You have the favor of your King.

Stand in humility and boldness and make your requests. Write your decrees. Wield the keys that God has given you as you watch at the gates like Mordecai and Nehemiah. Build the kingdom of God, with a "trowel" in one hand for building and a "spear" in the other hand to contend against the enemy (Nehemiah 4:17).

From the Heart of Father God

Do you hear the echo of Mordecai's question to Queen Esther in your spirit? It reverberates throughout the ages, in the synergy of the ages! I am calling you, My sons and daughters, for such a time as this! Do not back down and do not back up. Rise up and speak up! You have My righteousness through My Son and the righteous are as bold as a lion! Roar and roar some more by My Spirit!

I have mantled you as My Mordecais for this hour to nurture, equip and call forth the Esthers who need healing, protection and fresh courage in their appointed destinies. I have mantled you as Esthers, ones who have walked through the fires of adversity to come to a place of complete surrender. No longer concerned with your own preservation, you are willing to lay down your life to preserve others--and even a nation.

I will sovereignly you at the right place at the right time, to come before kings and speak My word and to appeal with humility but boldness. Nations are hanging in the balance and Hamans are hanging on the gallows. You are My end times warrior who has been appointed and anointed to turn back the battle at the gates and to release a stunning turning of tables in your own life and in the life of even your nation.

I am calling you as a deliverer to rise up in My Spirit and bring deliverance to every heart and every sphere that I position you in. For it's the greatest hour of My deliverance upon the earth and I am the God of the impossible! Allow Me to do the impossible in you and through you--for My glory and the harvest of souls that is here!

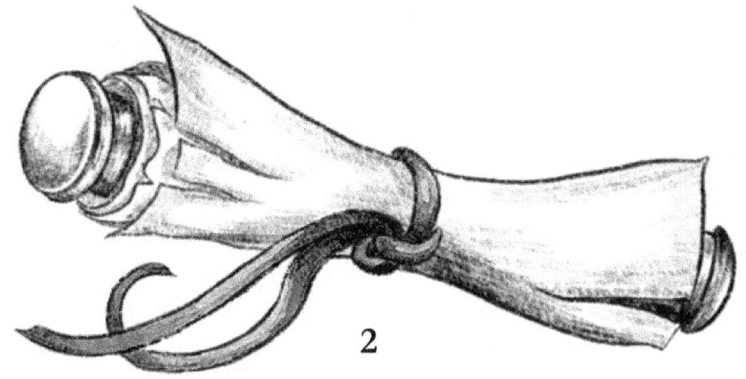

2

AN ANCIENT FOE

In this season of America, we are witnessing extraordinary justice being released. Justice is the "flip side" to judgment. *They are two edges of the same sword, two sides of the same coin--both sourced in God's love.* In the perfection of His love, God is exposing the "Hamans" that have been crafting evil schemes, many times covertly. This exposure comes for redemptive purposes.

We are witnessing these Hamans, sometimes even on the nightly news, fall one by one into their own carefully-arranged traps. The dam on the river of justice has broken and now it is flowing like a mighty river--and God's righteousness is rushing like a powerful stream (Amos 5:24).

This river of justice is like a thundering waterfall--picture the immense power and breathtaking majesty of Niagara Falls. That's a fitting description for the unstoppable power and love of God being released in His justice! Remember: His justice and judgment both come from His love, which is His very essence.

As a remarkable picture of this "waterfall of justice" in the natural, on Feb. 23, 2020 (just a few weeks before Purim), a tropical cyclone named *Esther* hit landfall in Australia. Esther was unusually slow-moving and doubled back to linger for nearly two weeks. This brought much-needed rainfall in abundance to a nation that had been wracked with prolonged drought and wildfires. Some said that they had been waiting ten years for rain like this.

Photos revealed stunning waterfalls that had been created because of the rainfall and overflow of this tropical cyclone Esther. One of them was a towering waterfall that looked like the veil of a bride that drapes all the way down to the ground and forms a pool of fabric.

Isaiah 44:3 says: "For I will pour water on him who is thirsty, and floods on the dry ground; I will pour My Spirit on your descendants, and My blessing on your offspring." The river and waterfalls of God's justice, even coming from the Mordecais and Esthers rising up, are thundering! The outpouring of His Spirit is upon us!

Thread of Justice

Justice is a thread woven into the Mordecai mantle that God is calling His ekklesia to in this hour of history. *God's ekklesia is essentially His government in the earth, His "called out ones".* If you are a born-again believer in Jesus Christ, you are a part of this ekklesia. God's heavenly government is being birthed into the earth realm in unprecedented ways. His government is an expression of His kingdom. We are His kingdom ambassadors.

The anointing of Holy Spirit that was upon Mordecai for the exploits he did in his day, is not only *upon* us it's *in* us! Holy Spirit is covering us afresh with this mantle today! This mantle is His manifest power. And it's a mantle for not only preserving the nation, but advancing it in its God-given destiny.

God has a destiny for America (and the nations) that is literally written in a book in heaven! Just as He had the answer in Esther's and Mordecai's day to preserve an entire nation facing death so that it can fulfill its rightful destiny--so He does today! You and I as kingdom ambassadors are a part of His solution! It's a life-or-death reality, but God is the Author of life and He is speaking "Life!" over America that drowns out the static of chaos and death.

Redemptive exposure is coming to those who are following in Haman's footsteps. *The snares of the enemy, so carefully laid, will end up being the gallows that the Haman spirit hangs on!* Sometimes plans craftily hidden for decades will unravel in a moment! Watch for these signs! This will not only bring freedom to the nation but also freedom to many who have been taken captive to do the enemy's will.

Many of those rescued will become primary leaders in this freedom movement, emptying the prisons of the enemy's camp. What an incredible turning of the tide! Once again, what God did miraculously in Esther and Mordecai's day He is doing today--and will continue to do through His sons and daughters!

At War with the Amalekites

Let's take a closer look at Mordecai and Esther's arch enemy, Haman. In Esther 3:6 we read: "Yet having learned who Mordecai's people were, he scorned the idea of killing only Mordecai. Instead, Haman looked for a way to destroy all of Mordecai's people, the Jews, throughout the whole kingdom of Xerxes." In this Scripture the demonic rage of Haman is exposed. It wasn't enough for him to try to exterminate only Mordecai, he took it to the extreme and sought to destroy *all* of the Jewish people in the kingdom.

This unquenchable anger, however, set in motion the unfolding of Haman's own destruction. He was overplaying his hand. He continued to plan and plot not just the killing of the Jews but pridefully crafting his own elevation. What he didn't know is how much he was setting the stage for his own destruction.

Haman was a descendant of a wicked Amalekite king named Agag--who is in the lineage of Esau. Here's the account of Agag: King Saul, Israel's first king, was told by the Lord to destroy the evil Amalekites. He only obeyed half-heartedly and allowed the Amalekite king to live. Because of his disobedience, he lost his kingship and the prophet Samuel ended up having to kill Agag. But King Agag's lineage continued--and centuries later, Haman came on the scene as his descendant.

The Amalekites represent the "pinnacle" of Israel's enemies. They were the first enemies that Israel faced when they came out of Egypt--and when they were about to possess the Promised Land after their 40 years in the desert. These are two critical junctures! Centuries later, they faced an Amalekite when they were in exile in Persia--Haman. Just like his ancestors, he was also seeking their destruction.

Fresh Strategy to Defeat an Ancient Foe

Take note of this: the Amalekite spirit is still moving through the generational lines and it's now operating through modern-day agents. This spirt wants to abort the destiny of a nation. It tried to stop the Israelites from coming out of captivity and then it tried to come against them when they were coming into their promise (Exodus 17:8-16)!

This is where we are in America right now. We are coming out of the captivity of a Babylonian structure that most of us didn't even know we were subject to. God has been speaking to me through Jeremiah 51 since 2017 and it is a chapter to pay attention to right now. We are coming out of Babylon and also poised to take possession of our promised land, our God-given destiny as a nation. But, there is an evil, Amalekite strategy to try to keep us from going out and keep us from coming in!

Like Joshua when he fought the Amalekites, we need a strategy to overcome this ancient demonic spirit. Moses directed Joshua and his men to war against Amalek while he stood on the mountain while Aaron and Hur held up his hands--and as long as he did that, Joshua had victory.

What a key time to raise up our hands like Moses the deliverer, and to raise our hands in praise! What a vital time for the Aarons and Hurs to come alongside the Moseses to help hold hands up!

In this hour, we need the Moseses and the Joshuas partnering as one! Generations aligning for victory! In many ways, this is a picture of what God did through Mordecai and Esther. God paired them up to bring a decisive turnaround and triumph to a nation facing existential threats!

Regarding the defeat of Amalek, consider Exodus 17:14-16: "Then the Lord said to Moses, 'Write this for a memorial in the book and recount it in the hearing of Joshua, that I will utterly blot out the remembrance of Amalek from under heaven.' And Moses built an altar and called its name, The-Lord-Is-My-Banner; for he said, 'Because the Lord has sworn: the Lord will have war with Amalek from generation to generation'". Incredible.

That name for the Lord is "Jehovah Nissi" which also means "God of miracles". He is our Banner, our covering, and He is our miracle-working God! It's time to see the miraculous manifest in your life and in your nation! Not only that, believe that the Lord *Himself* will war against the Amalek spirit from generation to generation! What a remarkable promise.

Root of Racism: Antisemitism

Haman has been systematically building gallows of evil under the radar (and now more overt) for decades in America through those aligned with this demonic spirit. This includes, but is not limited to, people driven by antisemitism. *Prophet Chuck Pierce teaches that the root of racism is antisemitism.* This is something to pause and reflect on, particularly as we have seen such racial division in our nation recently.

The good news is that God sees all of the enemy's tactics to destroy the nation from the inside out. He is *now* shining His light in a greater way on the enemy's plots, even in the halls of Congress. Additionally, *as antisemitism gets more brazen, this is backfiring on the enemy* and leaders are arising in bold authority to condemn antisemitism—for the whole world to take notice. Once again, we see the enemy overplaying his hand.

God calls us to love and bless Israel and the Jewish people and He also says He will curse those who curse them (Genesis 12:2-3). We need to take this seriously--and regularly invoke the blessings of Genesis 12:3 upon America.

Purim and Yom Kippur Connections

Ponder this connection: *Yom Kippur (the highest holy day for Jewish people) and Purim both have the word "pur" in them. This means "casting of lots"*. With Purim, the Jewish nation was in grave danger awaiting deliverance. At Yom Kippur, the Jewish nation was also in peril awaiting deliverance. The nation would essentially hang in the balance until the verdict of "not guilty" was given to the high priest and the sins of the nations were atoned for (Yom Kippur is also called the Day of Atonement). Do you see the connection? *Both Purim and Yom Kippur are connected to the deliverance and preservation of a nation.* Both of these also have elements of fasting, feasting and joy.

Watch how God brings unprecedented deliverance at Purim. And watch how His people respond with great, uncontainable joy!

From the Heart of Father God

My child, your enemies are ultimately My enemies. Have no fear. Many of the enemies you contend with are ancient enemies of even My people Israel. They are enemies of My covenant. And as I promised to be at war with the Amalekites from generation to generation, so I do for you. The enemies that have tried to stop you from going out and from going in, from walking out of captivity and from stepping into your inheritance, are not a threat to you because I am your Defender! I promised in my Word in Revelation 19:11 to judge and then make war on My enemies (your enemies)! I am now judging your enemies from my Courts in Heaven and I am making war on those who have sought to oppress, harm, steal and silence you.

My judgment is releasing justice to you and I promise to you that the thief must repay 7-fold. You are receiving more than 7-fold in this hour! Generational compensation and treasures are coming to you in unfathomable ways. My favor is increasing upon you, as it did for Mordecai and Esther. Spend this favor well. Invest it on behalf of others like my servants did and watch the abundant return on your investment. You will find that favor enlarging even as your tent pegs and your authority, your metron, enlarges.

I promise in My Word that the kingdoms of this world are becoming My kingdom (Revelation 11:15) and I am bringing this about through you, My kingdom ambassador on the earth! You are a key part in My ekklesia, my government, in the earth. Stand up and stand out and release My government in every sphere I call you to. Pray and war and worship from heaven to earth! Let your faith arise because triumph is at hand!

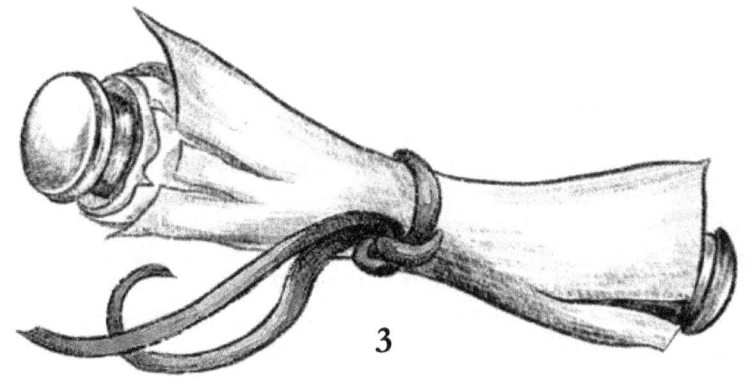

3

TRAUMA TO TRIUMPH

Let's take a trip back in time about 2,500 years. The Book of Esther begins in 483 B.C. The Jewish people had been living in exile for over 100 years, after being taken captive by King Nebuchadnezzar.

In this context, we learn of Mordecai, "son of Jair, the son of Shimei, the son of Kish, who had been carried into exile from Jerusalem by Nebuchadnezzar king of Babylon, among those taken captive with king Jehoiachin, king of Judah" (Esther 2:6). We discover that Mordecai had a cousin (most scholars believe they were first cousins) named Hadassah "whom he had brought up because she had no father or mother. This girl, who was known as Esther, was lovely in form and features, and Mordecai had taken her as his own daughter when her father and mother died" (vv. 7-8).

That's immeasurable trauma in many dimensions. *We're talking about an entire people group being ripped from their land and home and belongings, and thrust into a foreign land that's counter to their faith and beliefs.* Multiple generations living as captives. Think of the impact this must have had upon each heart and family--and the mindsets and identity that certainly developed around this reality. Not only this, Hadassah lost her parents and was orphaned. That's exponential loss and trauma.

This loss, brokenness and exile is picture of many modern-day sons and daughters in American culture because of generations of trauma and marital and family brokenness--and the fallout this creates. Millions of people do not have a father and mother in their lives or if they do, their parents are emotionally or physically (or both) absent. This is often cyclical and generational. They are living in "exile" to the "homeland" of what God designed for them to experience. Many are rootless and aimless, wandering the wasteland of our culture looking for who they are and a place to belong and to be loved.

Culture of Orphans

Countless people in American culture have no grid or experience of the genuine love and nurture of a father and mother, the safe womb that God designed for children to grow up in: spiritually, emotionally, mentally and physically. Instead, we have a culture of "practical" orphans who are crying out for belonging and significance and love--and finding it in destructive ways that the enemy presents to them as authentic. Sadly, it's a counterfeit of the real that only God offers.

It's not clear how Mordecai came to bring Hadassah up or even what that looked like on a practical level, but we do know that she had a serious need for a home, protection, love, parenting and more. Mordecai stepped up to the plate. We also don't know the age that he did this, but we do know that God equipped him to be a father to her. Some of you need to hear this.

You may feel that you're not old enough to father or mother someone spiritually, or you may feel that you're too old! It's not about your age. It's about your heart being willing to say a "divine yes" to the Lord when He calls you to help love an orphan into maturity. Remember that it's the Spirit of God dwelling in you that equips you to be able to do this--it's not anything you can do in your own wisdom or strength (Zechariah 4:6).

Your part may be a short-term investment of a few months of discipling a new believer, or coming alongside someone who is struggling to offer support. The foundation is the love of God. It could also be as long-term as actually adopting a child.

When legalized federally-funded abortion is finally eradicated in our nation (pray earnestly that it will!) there will be many pregnant mamas in need or in crisis who will require nurturing as they carry their children to term. There will be many more babies who will need loving adoptive homes and families to be placed into.

You may not be called to adopt, but there are countless practical ways that you can support these mamas and their babies. The Lord empowers you by His Spirit to release the spirit of adoption (Romans 8:15) to a world that desperately needs His heart expressed through the love of a spiritual father and mother.

The Secret of the Secret Place

A question, similar to the one that Mordecai posed to Esther, is: are you willing to say *yes* to God? No matter what? Even if great personal cost is involved? For some of you--perhaps even risking your life?

Do you know Father God and His heart and ways deeply enough in order to trust Him implicitly to say yes to Him? If you don't, then be encouraged that you can know Him and His love in a much deeper way! Even in the midst of the chaos around you, your heart can be at rest in Him. This is what you were made for. You were designed to live in and from the "secret place".

The secret place is essentially His presence. By His Spirit, you can live from that place of His presence as a lifestyle as you learn to live from your human spirit. Your spirit is the essence of who you are and where the Spirit of God dwells in you. You were made to experience a union, a oneness, with Father, Son and Holy Spirit. First Thessalonians 5:23 tells us that we are spirit, soul and body.

Be intentional about staying close to the Lord every day and say no to distractions. Talk with Him in prayer. He loves to hear your voice. Wait on Him. Listen to what He's saying to you—and do what He tells you to do out of your trust in Him. God speaks and you can hear His voice. Dig into the Bible—His love letter to you.

His Word is living and active and goes right to the heart (Hebrews 4:12). An intimate relationship with Him is what you were made for! Allow your heart to long for His presence. He longs to be with you too, His beloved child. *Knowing Him and being known by Him—and making Him known—these are the essentials.*

Intimacy Establishing Identity

From this place of continually receiving your Father's love, you will be rooted and established in His love and your identity will be formed and secure. In your intimacy and oneness with Him, your destiny will unfold. Your heart's desire will be to find ways, in the unique "language" that God has given to you, to make Him known. Remember that you are a carrier of His presence and His glory. His Word says that you are the light of the world and a city on a hill (Matthew 5:14). That is who you are!

As you draw near to Him, you will hear what's on His heart and mind-- and you can share from the depths of your heart, too. With the "first love" fires burning in your heart, you will experience a freedom and a fullness that is unparalleled. As you and the Lord "walk" together each day, He will prepare you "for such a time as this" to arise fearlessly and fulfill your destiny!

Where has God appointed you in this end times harvest field? He has appointments for you and ways to partner with Him and align with others that can literally shift your family, school, workplace, city—and even nation! As we will discover in the Book of Esther, this partnering with God not only brought preservation and tremendous advancement to Mordecai and Esther in their individual destinies, but to all of the Jewish people!

Divine Yes to God

It's time for the Mordecais in this hour of history to find fresh courage in their relationship with God and make a decision to boldly step up-- together! *The astonishing turnarounds in the Book of Esther are manifesting now in America, and the nations, and we are poised for even more.* Ultimately, these appointed turnarounds are setting the stage for this last great move of the Spirit of God on the earth. It's already here but this movement, this awakening, is gaining in momentum in ways we have never seen before. May each of our hearts be awake and ready!

Mordecai (and Esther) said yes to God, and look what transpired. Can you imagine if Mordecai hadn't said yes? The Jewish people at the time were facing a literal genocide. Ponder the significance of his divine yes to the Lord and the way it literally preserved a people group from extinction. *This altered not only the history of the Jewish people and Israel but the history of the world because God says that He chose Israel to be a blessing to all the nations of the earth (Genesis 12:2).*

Ultimately, "salvation is from the Jews" (John 4:22). Our Messiah, Yeshua (Jewish name for Jesus Christ), is Jewish of course! Out of His sacrificial love, He gave the ultimate yes to His Father God and laid down His very life for us. "By this we know love, because He laid down His life for us. And we also ought to lay down our lives for the brethren" (1 John 3:16).

Mordecai, a Jewish man living before the time of Yeshua, was also used by God to bring deliverance and to continue the lineage of the Jewish people so that, generations later, our Savior could be born into the earth, crucified on a cross for our sins and raised again to new life. Through Yeshua's body and shed blood, we are forgiven, saved, healed and delivered! Made completely new creations (2 Corinthians 5:17)! Not only that, we are His ambassadors of reconciliation and have been called to do even greater works than He did while on the earth (2 Corinthians 5:20; John 14:12)!

In the panorama of human history, consider how Mordecai's divine yes to the Lord has literally shaped your own history and personal story. Profound. *Your yes to Father God can also have this kind of weight--for generations to come.* Ponder that deeply. Your decisions now can affect not just your family and descendants but the *nations*. Who knows but that God has brought you to the kingdom for such a time as this? You were born to be a history-maker!

Raise Up the Orphans

God is looking for Mordecais, both male and female, who are willing to raise up those who have been orphaned (and this comes in many shapes and forms) like Esther in our society. Remember that this doesn't mean you need to be a "super saint". Simply put, you need to walk and talk with Jesus as a lifestyle and let Him love, empower and direct you.

There are hurting Esthers are everywhere. They need the love and direction of a Mordecai--someone who will stick with them in their tough times to remind them of who God says they are. This is not to suggest an unhealthy, codependent type of relationship, however. Esthers are not projects or people who need "fixing". Esthers are both men and women of all ages who need mature discipleship and genuine relationship from a pure heart, both truth and love, to help them fulfill the call of God on their lives--including the message they carry.

God is bringing Mordecais and Esthers together in a way that is holy and complementary. Mordecais are able to provide a "safe place" for Esthers to land because they know and receive the comfort of Holy Spirit as a lifestyle. They offer an opportunity for others to be genuinely seen and heard and known, and to be encouraged to grow into all that God has made them to be. For some, this may involve godly counsel and wisdom to help Esthers heal from their past wounds.

This can also include coaching, like a life coach who helps Esthers to dream and look forward into the future and hope that God has for them (Jeremiah 29:11). The Esthers need both perspectives. God is healing the "healers" and delivering the "deliverers" in this time of history. There is a whole generation of Esthers coming into the kingdom of God who will need this kind of healing and deliverance that is fostered in a variety of secure, godly relationships with mature believers.

Many of you Mordecais have been in an intense season of receiving your own healing and deliverance--even from the orphan spirit--in order to come into greater fullness of sonship (which of course applies to male and female). This healing is not just for you and your family. This is potentially for many people.

You have delegated authority as a believer in Yeshua, but your humble submission to God's process of preparation and your own journey of overcoming gives you *earned* authority and heavenly insight and wisdom. This is essential and life-giving to the Esthers that God brings into your life.

Beauty Treatments

Both Mordecai and Esther experienced intense preparation for the destiny that God called them to. Esther received one full year of "beauty treatments" and in many ways, this is symbolic of the preparation that Mordecai experienced as well. "Each young woman's turn came to go in to King Ahasuerus after she had completed twelve months' preparation, according to the regulations for the women, for thus were the days of their preparation apportioned: six months with oil of myrrh, and six months with perfumes and preparations for beautifying women. Thus prepared, each young woman went to the king, and she was given whatever she desired to take with her from the women's quarters to the king's palace" (Esther 2:12-13).

Esther had a total of 12 months of treatments. The number 12 is the number for God's government, the apostolic. Apostolic essentially means "to build the kingdom of God" and the word "apostle" means "sent one". Mordecai was very apostolic, which we will learn more about in other chapters, and teamed up with Esther to release the government of God, His kingdom, in their hour of history.

These 12 months of treatments weren't just about looking and smelling lovely. These were prophetic symbols of the spiritual purification that Esther submitted herself to, in order for the "government" of God to manifest in her life.

Myrrh is a costly oil representative of suffering. It is extracted from a tree and is sometimes called "tears from a tree". The perfumes are a picture of the "fragrance of heaven" that ultimately came forth from the purity of Esther's heart as she willingly laid down her life first to God and then for her people (which the "myrrh season" prepared her to do).

Mordecai laid down his life in a similar manner. They were both made ready for the crucial assignments the Lord had given to them.

Mordecai and Esther became a sweet-smelling sacrifice to the Lord. Ephesians 5:2 says: "And walk in love, as Christ also has loved us and given Himself for us, an offering and a sacrifice to God for a sweet-smelling aroma." In the Old Testament in Exodus 25, we see God instructing Moses with the pattern for the tabernacle and in verse 8 God says: "And let them make me a sanctuary, that I may dwell among them." Profound. Just a few verses prior, He gives these instructions: "oil for the light, and spices for the anointing oil and for the sweet incense" (v.6).

In this hour, Yahweh is giving us fresh oil for our lampstand and spices for this sacred anointing oil and the sweet incense. As His Bride we have become His sanctuary for Him to dwell, each of us His tabernacle on the earth. The perfume of heaven, even the incense of our prayer, is being released from us in greater dimensions. We are being made ready for the return of our Bridegroom-King!

Purification Nation

There is a whole company of Mordecais and Esthers going through their purification season in order that they can come forth radiant and shining forth the glory light of God in them. No leaven of Egypt. Flesh being removed. This purifying is preparation--to prepare the way of our coming King. Additionally, this absolutely must happen before the speaking forth and divine timing to go before leaders and kings of the earth, as some of you will be called to do.

The Lord Himself is sovereignly superintending this holy process for each of us. All that He asks for is our heart. When He fully has our heart, then submitting to this process is not burdensome. We gladly surrender to the One we know intimately and love--and trust.

Once again, Mordecai certainly had to submit to God's own "beauty treatments" and purification as well. You don't become a man with such integrity and governmental authority without first surrendering yourself to the Lord and the intense process this entails. Can you imagine what he had to overcome in his life?

He experienced the harsh realities of being an exile in a foreign land and serving a foreign king, in addition to protecting and caring for an orphaned relative positioned as a queen. Not to mention the fact that his evil enemy Haman sought to take his very life. All of this certainly brought manifold tests, trials and temptations. But Mordecai triumphed, by the Spirit of God, through it all.

Consider how much purification happened in Mordecai's life to be entrusted with the responsibilities that he carried--not to mention how he collaborated with his cousin-queen to see the preservation of an entire nation. *Many years of faithfulness and quiet obedience to God were the pathway to Mordecai's ultimate promotion* to second in command in the nation, bearing the king's signet ring, royal robe and royal horse.

Are you a Mordecai in this hour who has also willingly submitted to God's purification season, who will now be wise and patient in the process that the Esthers are experiencing? Your season of intense training and testing is now yielding a harvest--for the global harvest of souls! You have been prepared for promotion and you have also been prepared to help Esthers step into their destiny! As you move together, you will see God move in miraculous ways—in your home, city, state and even nation!

Trauma to Triumph

Ponder this: Esther was not just a beautiful young woman entered into some kind of "beauty contest" for the king. She was ripped out of the safety of her home and the Jewish way of life she undoubtedly grew up in. She was taken, like a hostage, to a completely different culture very opposite from her own. She was brought to the king's palace and made part of his harem. This is not romantic. This is human trafficking. Can you imagine the trauma that this young woman faced? All of this is in addition to her trauma from being orphaned.

The phrase "trauma to triumph" comes to mind as we look at Esther's storyline. She endured the intense grief and trauma of losing both of her parents and being an orphan. She was literally trafficked out of the safety of her home and culture as a young woman--forced into a culture completely opposite her beliefs. She was essentially made a part of a harem, made subject to those horrors. But, God sustained her through it all and undoubtedly gave much support, care and love through her cousin Mordecai who adopted her and eventually advised and counseled her as queen.

God prepared her, even though the immensely devastating events of her life to rise up as a deliverer for her entire nation. *Trafficked to triumph. Trauma to triumph!* Once again, triumph means more than winning the battle. It means victory *and* conquest over the enemy. In the same way, God prepared Mordecai, as one living in the midst of an exiled people, caring for his orphaned cousin and serving a foreign king, to overcome the pain and loss in his storyline and to be a deliverer of his people!

There is a similar call in this hour for the Mordecais and Esthers to arise. God has been preparing us through the difficulties in our storylines and the intensity of our warfare. *We've being going through a purification and preparation period, just like a bride does!* We are His Bride that is arising and shining forth His glory light. Delivered to be deliverers. Father God is turning our trauma into triumph. Personal turnaround in concert with territorial turnaround--even turnaround of an entire nation!

Jesus has freed us to go forth and be freedom fighters in our day. Contending in the spirit realm for both individual hearts and for our nation—and for Israel. God has also called America to arise boldly as an Esther in this hour to stand for, and stand with, our fellow covenant nation of Israel. Who knows, America, that God has called you to manifest the kingdom to the nations for such a time as this?

From the Heart of Father God

My Esthers are arising in this hour, but where are My Mordecais? Where are the spiritual fathers and mothers who have matured in their sonship to now be willing to adopt and nurture the orphans in the culture who have an Esther calling? Who will rise up and release My Father's heart and the spirit of adoption in the land? Where are the ones who will train and coach the orphans into their destiny? Where are the ones who will sacrificially lay down their lives, in little and big ways, in order to support the Esthers to arise and shine?

Where are the Mordecais who will selflessly "work for the good of all the people" in the nation, with no agenda of their own other than being about My business? Who will work for the good of others, regardless of ethnicity, gender, age or political party? Where are the ones with the integrity and uprightness to do this? Where are the Mordecais who have so given their heart to Me in their oneness with Me that My heart flows purely from their heart?

Where are my Mordecais and Esthers? Where are the those who are living from such a place of oneness in Me that nothing else truly matters? Where are those with dove's eyes with a singular focus on Me? I've been preparing my Esthers and my Mordecais in the fire of adversity and the daily persecutions. They've been overcoming their insecurities and fears. They have gone through the beautifying treatment of their souls, bringing deep purification and purging so they can radiate My glory.

The fiery trials don't burn them because they're already on fire for Me. They are rising up with fire in their eyes, My eyes. They are willing to do whatever it takes to see My love and power manifest in the earth and My kingdom established. They are My deliverers, even of nations. Watch as nations will be spared and preserved through My company of Mordecais partnering with the Esthers, burning with My love and power and demonstrating My kingdom wherever I plant them. Watch how I cause them to triumph in every sphere I place them in to demonstrate My glory.

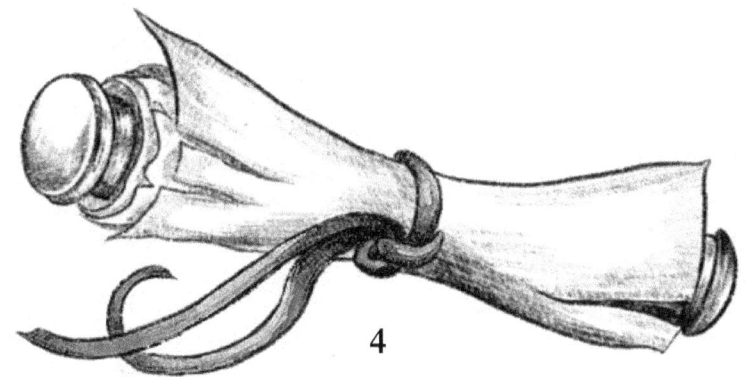

4

NEW APOSTOLIC ERA

As we look at Mordecai's life, once again we see a picture of an apostolic anointing. The "anointing" is the manifest power of God. Apostles appointed by God are sent by Him to build up people, cities and nations by building the kingdom of God from heaven to earth. Not all are called to be apostles, of course, but as believers each of us has an apostolic dimension to our lives to be His "sent ones" and to build the kingdom of God. Our Chief Apostle, our Head, is Yeshua!

The apostolic anointing is reflected in servant leadership: living selflessly for the welfare of others and seeking to equip and empower them to fulfill their God-given destiny. This is what apostles of God and apostolic believers do. It is living humbly in a "low" place as a foundation stone and a servant of all. The apostolic anointing is multi-dimensional, but one of the core aspects is being a spiritual father or mother. In Esther 2:23, we learn that: "every day Mordecai paced in front of the court of the women's quarters, to learn of Esther's welfare and what was happening to her." This is serious commitment to Esther's well-being.

Mordecai was not only a father to Esther, this experience groomed him to ultimately became a father to his nation. Consider that this same kingdom principle can apply to you. At the end of the Book of Esther, it states that Mordecai worked for the well-being of the people and spoke for the welfare of the Jews (Esther 10:3). He was faithful to work for the well-being of his cousin-daughter when he adopted her. Then, they were both promoted into the palace, and he continued to faithfully serve both Queen Esther and King Ahaseurus.

Eventually, this led to Mordecai being elevated to second in command to serve his *nation*--to be a father to his nation. When we are faithful with the "little" God gives us, He can entrust us with more. That is a kingdom principle (Luke 16:10) and we see this played out powerfully in Mordecai's life and legacy.

Mordecai flowed in this apostolic anointing as a lifestyle, and Esther was certainly watching and following his guidance--first and foundationally in the peace and safety of her home and ultimately in the crisis of a foreign palace. In Esther 2:20 we read: "She continued to follow Mordecai's instructions, just as she had done growing up".

This is echoed in the New Testament in a powerful way with Yeshua's words to us as His children: "My beloved ones, just like you've always listened to everything I've taught you in the past, I'm asking you now to keep following my instructions as though I were right there with you. Now you must continue to make this new life fully manifested as you live in the holy awe of God—which brings you trembling into his presence. God will continually revitalize you, implanting within you the passion to do what pleases him" (Philippians 2:12-13 TPT).

If I Perish, I Perish

Esther's willingness to ultimately come to a place of immense sacrifice for her people is heard in her bold statement, "If I perish, I perish". This was undoubtedly influenced greatly by observing how her cousin-father lived his life for God in private and in public--his integrity.

Esther proclaimed this statement of surrender after she had called for a three-day fast for herself, her maids and her people (Esther 2:15-16). Surely, fasting was something that had been woven into her upbringing--learned and modeled from Mordecai. *A core of the Mordecai mantle is living a lifestyle of prayer and fasting.*

In this moment of immense pressure on Esther, the years of training and instructing she experienced in her faith formation in the home resulted in precisely the right step to take in a moment of national crisis. She knew that the only hope for the Jewish people was to seek the face of God and His mercy through corporate prayer and fasting. In many ways, this call is playing out in our nation (and the nations) in our hour of history. Allow the Word of God and the Spirit of God to give you fresh revelation about the inherent power released through prayer and fasting--especially when it is corporate.

This process of maturing that Esther experienced is much like our own. It is forged in the slow, daily fires of dying to self. The stripping of the flesh. The laying down of a life for others through the sometimes-mundane circumstances in marriage, family, school, workplace and simply our daily interactions with others in the world. Every day brings opportunities to have our character refined and built.

Ultimately, submitting to God's refining process can lead to being one who will lay down his literal life. Esther, like Mordecai, eventually matured to a place where she was willing to give up her life in order to spare the life of her people.

We know that Yeshua is the ultimate example to us in this. "He existed in the form of God, yet he gave no thought to seizing equality with God as his supreme prize. Instead he emptied himself of his outward glory by reducing himself to the form of a lowly servant. He became human! He humbled himself and became vulnerable, choosing to be revealed as a man and was obedient. *He was a perfect example,* even in his death—a criminal's death by crucifixion! Because of that obedience, God exalted him and multiplied his greatness! He has now been given the greatest of all names!" (Philippians 2:6-9, TPT).

What about you? How has God been preparing you, though daily struggles and sometimes daunting tests and trials, to come to a place of complete abandonment to the Lord? It's laying it all down. It's a "low place" where you are willing to give everything you hold dear to the Lord, even your own life, out of radical trust in Him and loving obedience to Him.

This ultimately comes from deeply knowing Him and His heart, and knowing who you are and who you are not, in a real and tangible way. All of this is a gift of grace from Father God! Make it your holy pursuit to know Him and make Him known. There is abundant grace for you to do this.

Apostolic Anointing

The apostolic anointing also calls out the identity of others and helps place them into their position in the kingdom of God. Mordecai raised Esther. He knew her inside and out--her giftings and her weaknesses. Her passions and her pitfalls. Without his fathering, she undoubtedly wouldn't have been able to "cut it" in the pressures that she faced of being taken out of her family, home and culture--and transplanted, quite traumatically, into a foreign kingdom and the horrors she faced there.

Mordecai certainly knew how to speak the truth in love to Esther, as a good father does. He had wisdom from God to call forth the "true Esther", even in times of crisis that she faced. His courage and shrewdness helped her to "take her seat" and be positioned to not only spare her own life, but to spare the lives of all of her people.

Mordecai built up Esther. Again, one of the dimensions of the apostolic anointing is "builder". Apostolic believers love to build! They live to build up people, cities, communities, states and nations. They plant people into the rich soil of the kingdom where they can grow and thrive.

Certainly, one of the key ways Mordecai built up Esther was through his words. His exhortation in Esther 4:14 is a classic example of this. He was calling her higher in the midst of immense pressure.

Consider this passage that clearly highlights the apostolic anointing in Jeremiah 1:9-10: "Then the Lord put forth His hand and touched my mouth, and the Lord said to me: 'Behold, I have put My words in your mouth. See, I have this day set you over the nations and over the kingdoms, to root out and to pull down, to destroy and to throw down, to build and to plant.'" Incredible. God set Jeremiah over nations and kingdoms! He touched his mouth, which is the Hebrew word "pey"--also connected to a Hebrew letter. The numerical equivalent of the letter pey is 80.

Decade to Decree and Declare

In the fall of 2019, we shifted into new Hebraic year of 5780 and the new Hebraic decade of the 80's--connected to the Hebrew letter pey, which means "mouth". Imagine the prophetic implications of an entire decade that is connected to speaking, expressing through the mouth, prophesying, praying, singing and more. It's a key decade to watch the gate of our mouths and to declare and decree "on earth as it is in heaven".

We are made in God's image and our words truly do have the power of life and death (Proverbs 18:21). *Therefore, we are either creating or destroying through our words. Think of this!* God has given us His creative power; therefore, our words actually create our world. Science even verifies this. This is sobering--but also empowering. Speak LIFE! Agree and align with Father, Son and Holy Spirit and release that through your words, especially your decrees and declarations in this Hebraic decade of the 80's!

In the Jeremiah 1 passage, the Lord touches Jeremiah's mouth. The words of God Himself flow through the prophet to pull down, destroy and throw down--and build and plant. This "twin anointing" of tearing down and then building is precisely what the apostolic anointing does.

Mordecai was set over a nation and a kingdom and through the very words of God in his mouth, he tore down what the enemy was plotting for destruction against Esther and the king he served. Additionally, through his words, he built up his cousin Esther, his king and ultimately, his nation and its destiny.

Foundational Equippers

Apostles are equippers. They equip people to do the works of the kingdom and to fulfill their destiny. Mordecai equipped Esther in his home and this set the stage for him to equip her in the palace. This is how it works for us as well. It starts in the altar of our own heart and then in the altar of our home and family. As we are faithful with these altars, the Lord can then entrust us to more and enlarge our territory.

Mordecai received his equipping from God and then was called to equip his cousin under his care with the wisdom and practical understanding she needed. This was for her to not only survive as an exile and a young girl in a harem--but to thrive in the purposes that God had for her, even as a queen of a foreign kingdom.

Apostles are also foundational. Ephesians 2:20 says that the church is built upon the foundation of the apostles and prophets, with Jesus as the Chief Cornerstone. Therefore, the apostolic anointing that God graced Mordecai with is foundational. It's what the rest is built on top of. If the foundation is "off" the whole building is crooked. So, it is with the Mordecai mantle.

What we do with this apostolic anointing is foundational, so our foundations need to be completely plumb lined to the Word of God. Ultimately, it is vital for us to be firmly rooted and established in the love of our Father God as His sons and daughters (Ephesians 3:17).

This apostolic anointing is empowering an entire generation as Mordecais to come alongside the Esthers and call them forth in their identity and destiny. As we look at Esther's life, we can see this apostolic anointing flowing through her as well. Consider that Jewish tradition even lists her and Mordecai as prophets. So, here we have a powerful example of the apostolic and prophetic working together to form that Ephesians 2:20 foundation. The power of God manifested in this foundation is literally what preserved an entire nation from extinction.

God is doing the same in this hour of history as He is bringing forth many fresh manifestations of the apostolic and prophetic anointings working in tandem to build the kingdom of God--upon the Chief Cornerstone of Yeshua! This inherently displaces the false foundations. They are shaking and coming down as the *true* foundations are being established in every sphere in our nation--and in the nations!

New Apostolic Era

On October 31, 2017 God spoke to me that the ekklesia crossed over a threshold into a new era: a new apostolic era. This converged with the 500th anniversary of the Reformation. I released this word at a small, but weighty, gathering at the apostolic center I am a part of, Josiah Center in St. Paul, MN.

We knew, even that night, that we were standing in a demarcation moment in the history of the Church: *"Tonight we are literally standing at the threshold of a new era in the Church, a new order of the government of God, a New Reformation. It's an awakening to our identity as kings and priests unto God. Coupled* with a resurgence of God's Word, we are receiving fresh, heavenly revelation and scrolls that will catalyze the Third Great Awakening and global harvest that has already begun. We get the privilege of being forerunners in this global shift taking place from institutional Christianity to the KINGDOM. The kingdom of God is within you, Revolutionaries, and the kingdom of God is at hand! Instead of one man driving one nail into the door of a church [Martin Luther], we are now the One New Man that God is driving like a vav or a stake from heaven to earth to mark the beginning of a new order in the Church, His government manifesting on the earth. This is not just reformation, this is revolution! We are end times revolutionaries!"

From the Heart of Father God

My child, it is My good pleasure to give you My kingdom. It is My delight that you are a co-heir with My Son. My heart is reaching out to you continually to come closer, to know Me and My heart deeper and deeper. I am constantly delighting in you as My child and who I made you to be. Did you know that I sing a song of love over you day and night? I am a warrior in your midst and I rejoice over you with joyful singing. I quiet your heart with My perfect, pure love (Zephaniah 3:17). Receive My love for you afresh today and allow your heart to be at rest in My love. You are loved, always and no matter what, with My everlasting love.

As you are continually filled and empowered in My love and mature to a place of spiritual father or mother, I call you forward. Will you step out? This Third Great Awakening will not be aborted if the fathers and mothers arise apostolically to be the foundation and to be the builders and the nurturers, the coaches and the disciplers. Bow your heart low in humility so you can soar high with Me! Build in My strength! Build up those around you in My love and power. Demonstrate My kingdom! Build My kingdom with Me, with joy, innovation and creativity in every sphere I've called you to! Be free to have fun with Me and be child-like because you are My dearly loved child!

In my Name, call forth the angelic council to open up over the apostolic and prophetic councils that I appoint you to. Collaborate and synergize in a new way with the angelic host to accomplish what I have marked out for you. Align your heart and your mind and your mouth with who I am and what I say in my Word! Decree my Word! Come closer to know Me in a greater way and know who you are and who I have called you to be.

I have fresh expressions of the apostolic and prophetic to align in new ways in this hour, to bring true foundations that displace the old, false foundations. This will bring unprecedented unlocking! Seek My face daily in intimacy and you will discover these new expressions. I will give you heavenly blueprints and wisdom regarding how and with whom to build them. You will not grow weary in well doing as you draw from the deep wells of My presence within you each day! You are soaring from glory to glory in Me!

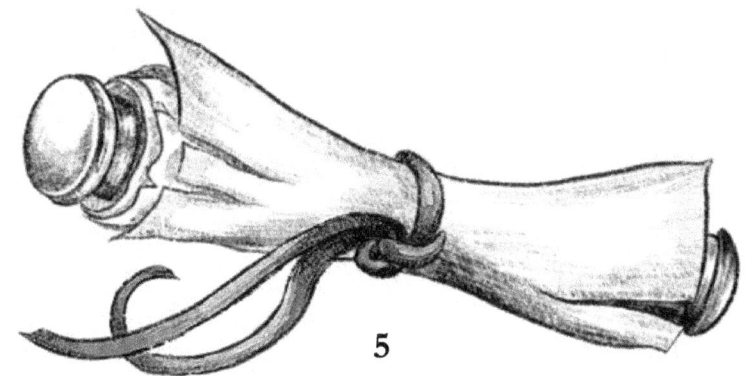

5

THE WARRIOR AND THE HIDDEN STAR

Our names hold great significance. One of the meanings of Mordecai's name is "warrior". What a prophetic namesake! God raised up an apostolic, prophetic warrior to stand boldly for his God and his nation. Mordecai did this in his God-given identity and authority, bringing about the defeat of not only an evil leader, but the overarching evil agenda designed to annihilate an entire nation. Warriors must first know their God and know themselves--and know their enemies.

Consider this powerful promise from Proverbs 21:22 (TPT): "A warrior filled with wisdom ascends into the high place and releases regional breakthrough, bringing down the strongholds of the mighty." Incredible. We are warriors in God's army *and* we need wisdom from above--always! We receive this as we ascend into the "high place" and "come up higher" (Revelation 4:1) through the open door in heaven.

In this crucial hour of history, we cannot afford to be warriors without wisdom. It's imperative for us to stand in the council of the Lord and to receive understanding that is pure. Listen to this description the Shulamite has of her Bridegroom in Song of Songs 5:12 (TPT): "He sees everything with pure understanding. How beautiful his insights—without distortion. His eyes rest upon the fullness of the river of revelation, flowing so clean and pure." All of this is our inheritance as the sons and daughters of God with His Spirit dwelling in us richly! May we access our inheritance in greater ways in this new era of history in order to build the kingdom of God and arise as the great warriors we are destined to be!

Praise is a Weapon

As Prophet Chuck Pierce's book title states, we "ascend in worship and descend in war". *One of our greatest weapons as warriors is worship and praise of our great King!* As we continue to get a deeper revelation of this by the Spirit of God, we will transform into a people living a lifestyle of praise--and transform the world around us! Nothing routs the enemy quicker than praise, which is why "Judah goes first" (Judges 20:18)! It's an hour when the "Judah" in our spiritual DNA is coming out of us: the warring, governmental, apostolic and roaring lions of praise that we are. And the enemy hears and runs away in fear!

Listen to this exhortation and let your spirit ascend: "Lift up a great shout of joy to the Lord! Go ahead and do it—everyone, everywhere! As you serve him, be glad and worship him. Sing your way into his presence with joy! And realize what this really means—we have the privilege of worshiping the Lord our God. For he is our Creator and we belong to him. We are the people of his pleasure. You can pass through his open gates with the password of praise. Come right into his presence with thanksgiving. Come bring your thank offering to him and affectionately bless his beautiful name!" (Psalm 100:1-4 TPT).

The Mordecai Mantle

What is the Mordecai "mantle"? A mantle has many layers of meanings. In its most basic form, it speaks of an outer garment, particularly used in ancient times, that would protect from the elements (Ezra 9:5). In can also be referred to as a robe or cloak. In Bible times, *prophets would sometimes wear a mantle which represented their authority given to them by God--a sign of God's covering and glory upon them.*

Perhaps the most notable example of a mantle is Elijah's cloak, or mantle, that was passed on to Elisha. "He also took up the mantle of Elijah that had fallen from him, and went back and stood by the bank of the Jordan. Then he took the mantle of Elijah that had fallen from him, and struck the water, and said, 'Where is the Lord God of Elijah?' And when he also had struck the water, it was divided this way and that; and Elisha crossed over" (2 Kings 2:13-14).

Ultimately, the mantle can also represent the anointing of God. Once again, this is the manifest power of God upon a believer. Therefore, the Mordecai mantle, the mantle that was upon Mordecai to be and to do all that God appointed for him, essentially was the anointing of God. How remarkable to consider that God's Spirit is now not only *upon* us as Spirit-filled believers in Jesus, but *within* us! (I Corinthians 3:16).

Coming Out of Hiddenness to Shine

Although this book is about Mordecai, it's important to understand more about his fellow nation-changer, too, because their storylines are so intertwined. Esther's name means both "hidden" and "star". In her life, we can see how she was hidden for a time, but came forth to shine like a star-- in God's timing. This is important to keep in mind. God knows your appointed time to come out of hiddenness.

The same can be said for Mordecai. He was quietly performing his duties at the king's gate and in due time, he ended up being promoted and displayed in a stunning way. He received the king's royal robe, horse and signet ring— and was profoundly and publicly honored and recognized! As we follow Yeshua wholeheartedly with wisdom and discernment, *we will be hidden when and where He calls us to be hidden and seen when and where He calls us to be seen.*

We don't need to promote ourselves; God is the one who promotes us! We also don't need to be afraid to stand up and stand out! We have been crowned with God's glory and honor as His Bride (Psalm 8:5). We have been called to shine like stars in the universe holding forth the word of LIFE to a crooked and depraved generation (Philippians 2:15). Shine! Release the glory light of God within you and bring God's Word of life in the midst of darkness! This is who you are!

John the Baptist/Elijah Anointing

This "coming out of hiding" that Esther experienced is similar to the prophets Elijah and John the Baptist. They were both hidden by God for a season of intense preparation, but then they came forth in full strength at the appointed time. Right on time! The intersection of eternity and time regarding these prophets' destinies and the destiny of their nation is remarkable. And in each case, the nation shifted radically!

This Elijah/John the Baptist anointing from God is what He is again bringing forth in this hour in His people. This is a forerunning anointing that goes ahead to prepare hearts and to prepare the way of the Lord. Our Bridegroom-King is coming! May we be a Bride who is made ready and prepared, eagerly awaiting the return of her Bridegroom.

Malachi 4:5-6 says, "Behold, I will send you Elijah the prophet before the coming of the great and dreadful day of the Lord. And he will turn the hearts of the fathers to the children, and the hearts of the children to their fathers, lest I come and strike the earth with a curse." This turning of hearts, of children to their fathers and the fathers to their children, is foundational amidst all of the brokenness in families. And, even more, this turning of hearts of children to their Father God is the centerpiece of this new move of God.

The Third Great Awakening is essentially about Father God and His love being released and received by multitudes who are awakening to Him and His love. Salvation, healing and deliverance coming to millions of souls hungry for the love and power of their Abba Father!

Many hearts are now awakening to the immeasurable love their Creator, Father God, has for them and responding with a true turning away from sin and wholehearted turning to Him. As God's ambassadors of reconciliation, we receive the honor to re-present Father God and His heart to them (2 Corinthians 5:18)! Consider this powerful description of the John the Baptist anointing: "He will also go before Him in the spirit and power of Elijah, 'to turn the hearts of the fathers to the children,' and the disobedient to the wisdom of the just, to make ready a people prepared for the Lord" (Luke 1:17).

The Elijah/John the Baptist anointing is to make ready a people prepared for the Lord! In John 1, some Jewish leaders were interrogating John and when they asked him who he was, he replied: "I am fulfilling Isaiah's prophecy: 'I am an urgent, thundering voice shouting in the desert—clear the way and prepare your hearts for the coming of the Lord Yahweh!'" (v. 23, TPT). This is where we are in the Church! God is releasing His urgent, thundering voice through a Bridal company of forerunners! We are trumpeting this wake-up call for hearts to be prepared for the coming of the Lord! Behold, the Bridegroom King is coming! Let all be made ready!

This is what the friends of the Bridegroom, the John the Baptists of this hour, cry out with all of their hearts. They are appointed messengers of the Lord with this holy message. John 1:6-9 in the Passion Translation reads: "Then suddenly a man appeared who was sent from God, a messenger named John. For he came to be a witness, to point the way to the Light of Life, and to help everyone believe. John was not that Light but he came to show who is. For he was merely a messenger to speak the truth about the Light. For the Light of Truth was about to come into the world and shine upon everyone." Is your spirit burning as you read this? This is describing who *you* are!

Myrtle Tree of Life

Esther's Jewish name was Hadassah, which means "myrtle". This evergreen shrub with petite white flowers and fragrant oil is thought to be a symbol of love or marriage. This sounds like a bride! How powerful to consider that imagery in the overall context of the Book of Esther. *God's chosen, purified Bride whom He brings to royal position as His Queen, also stands ready to lay down her life for her people.* The delicate white flowers speak of her purity and the fragrant oil symbolizes the anointing of Holy Spirit and perfume of heaven upon her.

Hadassah also possesses the virtues like the Shulamite in the Song of Songs. Similarly, she bears the characteristics of the "radiant bride" mentioned in Proverbs 31:16-20 in the Passion Translation. Remember that as we speak of the Bride, we are speaking of both male and female, the sons and daughters of God. Therefore, these characteristics apply to not only Esther, but Mordecai.

"She sets her heart upon a nation and takes it as her own,
carrying it within her.
She labors there to plant the living vines.
She wraps herself in strength, might, and power in all her works.
She tastes and experiences a better substance,
and her shining light will not be extinguished,
no matter how dark the night.
She stretches out her hands to help the needy
and she lays hold of the wheels of government.
She is known by her extravagant generosity to the poor,
for she always reaches out her hands to those in need."

This is a beautiful portrait of Esther/Hadassah and Mordecai as they carried a nation within them—and a stunning description of the Bride of Christ in this hour. See yourself in these powerful promises! Set your heart upon your nation and take it as your own. Take ownership and responsibility. Sound your note in the orchestra and "plant the living vines".

Stretch out your hands to help those in need--they are everywhere, especially in the crises facing our nation. Release the fruit of Holy Spirit where God has sovereignly positioned you as a "myrtle tree" of God's love. Allow the fragrance of the anointing oil of Holy Spirit upon you to diffuse into every atmosphere you step into. Be the life-giver whom God has called you to be!

Favor, Favor, Favor

A resounding theme of the Book of Esther is favor. Mordecai and Esther were greatly favored. They had favor wherever they went to fulfill the destiny God had given them. In Esther 2:15b we read: "And Esther obtained favor in the sight of all who saw her." That is stunning favor that comes only from the hand of God. Consider that we, as the Bride of Christ, are in a similar hour. God is pouring out his favor! What joy! As we receive it, may we seek Him for great wisdom to spend it wisely.

God's lavish favor is not just for our benefit but for the benefit of others--even our nation. "And the king said to her, 'What is it, Queen Esther? What is your request? It shall be given you, even to the half of my kingdom'" (Esther 5:3). Our King Jesus is asking us, His Bride, the same question today: "What is your request?" It's time for us to ask BIG and to make bold petitions of our King! It's time for the Bride to arise in the favor of the Lord and to spend the currency of our favor, even for our nation's turnaround.

From the Heart of Father God

You are My precious child and you are My Son's radiant Bride. You are chosen, blessed and highly favored--at all times. I am pouring out My favor upon you in this hour. I have already given you My kingdom. Now go into the highways and byways and stretch out your hand to those who need Me. Be My hands and feet. Display My glory and demonstrate My kingdom. This is the hour of the greater works of My Son that you shall do--as He is so are you in the world (I John 4:17). There are times when you are hidden, but trust My timing for your revealing. You are My shining star, wherever you are--whether interceding in a prayer closet or preaching to the masses. Allow Me to position and promote you--My ways are always the best for you, so you can trust Me.

Receive My pure love each day, like a nourishing meal to your spirit. Then, carry and release My Father's heart to a world that is starving for love--simply by being who I have made you to be. You have the honor of re-presenting Me. Through you and the forerunner anointing I have given you; I am turning the hearts of the children back to Me, their Father. I'm also turning earthly fathers' hearts back to their children and their children's hearts back to their fathers. It's a glorious return to original intent. Go forth in the anointing of My servants John the Baptist and Elijah. You are making ready a people prepared for My Son, your Bridegroom-King coming back soon.

Allow your spirit to ascend higher in Me. Release praise to Me in all circumstances and watch the enemy flee! You are My appointed worshipping warrior in this hour! Ask Me for wisdom daily and you will rise into the high places and the strongholds of the enemy will be dismantled! My light and My sound are within you, so allow them to come forth in creative expressions in praise and worship! Sing as a king, to me your Great King! I have crowned you with My glory and honor.

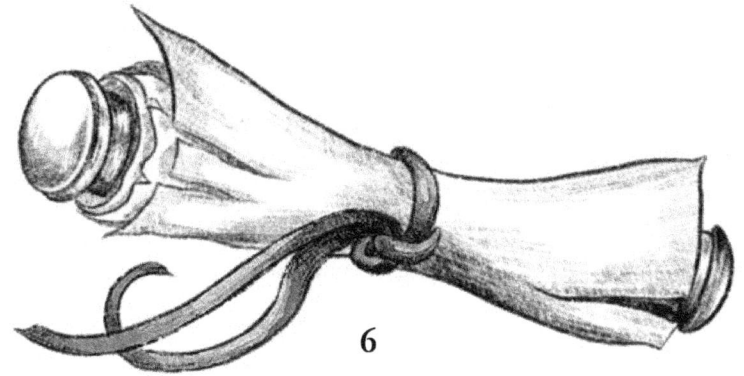

6

WRITE A NEW DECREE

The spirit realm, in a foundational way, involves what is legal and illegal. The enemy is the ultimate legalist, so he will look for any way he can to accuse you. If he can't find any "dirt" on you, he is fully willing to look into your generational lines to see if there is iniquity (generational sin) that he can use as a case against you. He is not just our adversary; he is an opponent in a lawsuit.

In Luke 18:3 we read: "Now there was a widow in that city; and she came to him, saying, 'Get justice for me from my adversary.'" That word "adversary" is the Greek word "antidikos". This term essentially means an adversary in a lawsuit or a courtroom. This is an important point as we look at the account of Mordecai and Esther.

Our spiritual adversary cunningly tries to change times and law (Daniel 7:25). This is precisely what Haman did with the king's decree to destroy the Jewish people. Decrees are like a court order. Haman tricked the king into signing this legal decree--he was deceptively going about this in a legal way, out of his demonic rage against Mordecai.

Here is the scenario: "Then the king's scribes were called on the thirteenth day of the first month, and a decree was written according to all that Haman commanded—to the king's satraps, to the governors who were over each province, to the officials of all people, to every province according to its script, and to every people in their language. In the name of King Ahasuerus it was written, and sealed with the king's signet ring. And the letters were sent by couriers into all the king's provinces, to destroy, to kill, and to annihilate all the Jews, both young and old, little children and women, in one day, on the thirteenth day of the twelfth month, which is the month of Adar, and to plunder their possessions. A copy of the document was to be issued as law in every province, being published for all people, that they should be ready for that day" (Esther 3:12-14).

It's nearly impossible to imagine such a decree. This decree conveys total destruction and annihilation of the Jewish people: men, women and little children. Can you imagine being a Jewish person reading a copy of that document--essentially your death sentence? All because of one wicked man's insidious desire to be worshipped was spurned.

Thanks to Esther's wisdom in hosting the two banquets with him and Haman, the king saw Haman's murderous intent to destroy all of the Jewish people--including Esther--in plain sight. He was incensed and moved to take swift action. He needed to take legal action because the original decree the king wrote could not legally be revoked.

Rise Up and Fight

A new decree had to be written to override the evil decree. This is precisely what Esther and Mordecai were tasked with writing. The decree equipped the Jewish people to bear arms and fight--legally! The Jewish people weren't just automatically saved from destruction. They had to fully engage in their process of deliverance, in the same way that Mordecai and Esther had to stand up courageously as deliverers. This is God's wisdom in calling out the warrior in them.

As America (and Israel) faces some of the same existential threats that the Jewish people faced in Esther's time, so we need to get in the game. We have to take personal responsibility in every dimension that God calls us to. We need to "bear arms" in the spirit realm with the spiritual weapons of warfare that God has given to us to defeat the enemy. Once again, one of our greatest weapons is praise! Praise terrifies the enemy!

Although the Jewish people had been exiles for generations in the time of Mordecai and Esther, this "exile attitude" and "slave mentality" had to be shed like an old coat--quickly. Having to rise up and fight for the preservation of your family and nation is one sure way to rid yourself of old mindsets!

Can you relate to this? Have you been living in a slave mentality although you know that God has already set you completely free through His Son Yeshua? You may know you are free, but are you ready to take the next step to believe what God says and *live* fully free?

Are you living like an orphan when you have already been made a son or daughter of the Most High God? Is it time to take off that old coat of myopic thinking and small living and instead believe God's Word that you are dressed in a royal robe of Christ's righteousness? Is it time to stop asking for what you have already received in the finished work of Jesus Christ?

Is it time to say a louder "no" to idolatry or compromise? Are you ready to stand up against the Haman spirit in your life that is trying to manipulate and annihilate you? Are you ready to see favor unleashed in your life and be promoted into positions and places you never imagined? Yeshua declared on the cross, "It is finished!" So, let's resolve to believe this and live fully free as His sons and daughters! He gets great glory when we do this!

5780-89: Decade of the Decree

Regarding the decrees: have you discovered "evil decrees" that the enemy has written against you or your ancestors that you see play out as generational patterns of sin (iniquity)? Be encouraged that you can write a new decree! You can override what the enemy has attempted to do, even for decades in your family line, by agreeing with and decreeing what God in heaven says! Agree and decree! You are empowered to be more than a conqueror to rise up and fight and defeat the enemy—not just for your generational lines and family but for the next generations coming after you!

There are many books of biblical decrees available now on the market and others that teach you how to write your own decrees. The best place to start, of course, is the Word of God. Identify Scriptures that are personal to you or specific to the situations you are facing. Write out the Scripture and *speak it out loud* as a decree! It's that simple!

Do you believe that the power of life and death is in the tongue (Proverbs 18:21)? Do you believe that His Word is alive, powerful and sharper than a double-edged sword (Hebrews 4:12)? Then, it's important to speak the Word of God aloud! You are created in the image of God and He has given you creative power with your words! Use your words wisely and well--they create! This is profound.

We are now in a time when we need to open up our mouths and decree what will be-- according to the Word of God. As the ekklesia, the government of God, it's time to rise up in our delegated and earned authority. We are authorized by the eternal Judge of all. As I noted previously, the fall of 2019 marked the turning of the page on a new Hebraic year and decade. Again, the decade of the 80's is connected to the Hebrew letter pey which has the numerical value of 80. Pey means "mouth, speak, expression". It is truly a Decade of the Decree!

There are Courts of Heaven strategies coming for the people of God in this hour to deal legally with the enemy's legal claims against them or their generational lines. God is bringing forth fresh revelation of the Courts of Heaven for us, as His ekklesia in this hour, to win in the Courts of Heaven. The prolific Daniel 7:22 Turnaround Verdict, which the Lord issued in 2014, has been trumpeted and prophesied by Prophets Jon and Jolene Hamill for several years and it is manifesting in profound ways in this time of history!

Daniel 7:22 declares: "until the Ancient of Days came, and a judgment was made in favor of the saints of the Most High, and the time came for the saints to possess the kingdom." This is a stunning picture of what transpired in Mordecai and Esther's day--and what God is releasing right *now* for the United States of America! And for the Jewish people and Israel! The Turnaround Verdict is being completed by the hand of God through His ekklesia! We don't know precisely what this turnaround looks like, but we can agree with God and decree this verdict!

Three Branches of Ekklesia

As we talk about the Courts of Heaven, keep in mind that there are three branches in the *heavenly government*. Isaiah 33:22 says: "For the Lord *is* our Judge, the Lord is our Lawgiver, the Lord is our King; He will save us". In this Scripture we see the judicial branch, the legislative branch and the executive branch. Of course, these are the basis for our 3-branched American government.

Consider that these branches also reflect us, the ekklesia, as the government of God on the earth! The judicial is represented by the prophetic role, the legislative is represented by the priestly function and the executive is represented by the kingly dimension. This is who we are!

The Church overall has been primarily functioning in the priestly role, which is essentially representing the needs of people to God. Recently, God has been reviving the kingly role for His people, bringing forth fresh revelation about this dimension of who we are. Rick Ridings, apostolic/prophetic leader who leads a house of prayer in Jerusalem, released a word in 2012 about a Crown and Throne movement that is about the reclaiming of the kingly dimension of believers.

Prophets Jon and Jolene Hamill, based out of Washington D.C., are leading this charge and wrote a book in 2013 in connection to this aptly titled *Crown and Throne*. It not only captures much of the essence of this movement, it is filled with key prophecy for America. Years later, much of this prophecy in their book has come to pass!

Righteous Judges

The Word of God declares that we are priests and kings unto Him (Revelation 1:6), which of course includes the legislative and executive heavenly branches of government. But, for several years now, the Lord has been highlighting to me the restoration of the third branch: the judicial. This is connected to the prophetic, as the judges of old like Samuel and Deborah were prophets. There is much revelation to be mined in all of this! We are his "judges", the third branch of the ekklesia on the earth.

Restore Your Judges

Another example of righteous judging: God appeared to King Solomon in a dream and essentially said, "What can I give you?" Solomon replied: "Therefore give to Your servant an understanding heart to judge Your people, that I may discern between good and evil. For who is able to judge this great people of Yours?" The speech pleased the Lord, that Solomon had asked this thing" (1 Kings 3:9-10).

Solomon asked for an understanding heart to judge God's people--and God was very pleased by this request! We are called to do the same today: to exercise righteous judgment with an understanding heart. This is greatly needed in this hour of history! The word "thresh" means "judge" which denotes separating. We are called to separate good from evil, light from darkness, in this hour with so much mixture. This separating process actually begins *within* us, as we allow the Word of God to separate between soul and spirit (Hebrews 4:12), so that we can live and move from our spirit—in submission to Holy Spirit.

In 2013, God encountered me with Isaiah 1:26 which has become an "inheritance verse" or "life verse" for me: "I will restore your judges as at the first, and your counselors as at the beginning. Afterward you shall be called the city of righteousness, the faithful city." When I read the verse, I knew that God was not only speaking about the earthly judicial system (which certainly needs restoration) but He was also speaking about His people sitting as "judges as at the first". This is a profound return to original intent!

Justice is the theme of the hour. *And we have been given the anointing of God to be His government on the earth, including a judicial dimension.* It's time to judge rightly, to discern correctly. John 7:24 commands: "Do not judge according to appearance, but judge with righteous judgment." It's time for us to bring forth righteous judgment, not demonic, fleshly judgment. To make righteous judgments in order to execute God's justice in our spheres.

You're a History Maker!

We need to, as Apostle Dutch Sheets says, "Put yourself in the storyline". We are truly in history-making, history-shaping times, which means we are history-makers and history-shapers! It's similar to the Revolutionary War when the common people, even though most undoubtedly didn't want to go to war, chose to rise up. They had to come out of their comfort zones and become warriors. They had to take responsibility.

Ordinary farmers were the bulk of this army and many pastors became "commanders" as their flock transformed into a platoon. Think of the courage these men had to have. Virtually no training. Ill-equipped and unprepared. But, they rose up *as one* and with the help of a sovereign, supernatural God and His angelic host, they won the war against the greatest empire of the day! A covenant nation was secured and miraculously birthed!

This is why the flag that the Revolutionary War soldiers flew in battle and on the naval ships said "Appeal to Heaven". They knew that their only hope was God and they boldly, humbly appealed to Him for the victory! If you are not familiar with the story behind the Appeal to Heaven flag, I highly encourage you to read the book by the same name, *An Appeal to Heaven*, written by Dutch Sheets. It's not just inspiring, it's a prophetic picture of where we are today!

Bottom line: the enemy knows his time is short and so an unquenchable rage has been set into motion. He wants to not only destroy believers in Christ but the entire nation of America with its covenantal roots and foundation in God. He knows what a domino effect this would have on the nations. Of course, the enemy's ancient quest to destroy Israel and Jewish people has also played out over millennia. But the enemy is overplaying his hand. God knows the end from the beginning and victory is already secured!

What the enemy is attempting to do is backfiring on him! And one of Yeshua's primary solutions in this hour is His humble yet bold, warring Bride who is standing alongside Him triumphantly to make history and see His destiny for nations fulfilled. It's about this end times harvest of souls! He says: "Ask me to give you the nations and I will do it, and they shall become your legacy. Your domain will stretch to the ends of the earth" (Psalm 2:8 TPT).

From the Heart of Father God

Beloved, you truly are part of My government on the earth. You are My righteous king, priest and judge. I am teaching and training you how to walk and manifest these three heavenly branches of government. I am calling you close to Me and My heart so that you make righteous judgments in this hour, because I promised in My Word that I would turn the hearts of the disobedient to the wisdom of the just.

I am restoring My judges as at the first (Isaiah 1:26). I am releasing My justice and you are My agent of justice in this hour. In My justice, I make right what has been wrong. I am doing this for you and through you. Watch as the dam breaks on My river of justice that flows from My throne! Watch how this waterfall of justice will sweep away much of what the enemy has been using to hold you back. Watch what I do in the nations to make what is wrong, right! This is part of my sweeping move to restore to original intent.

You are called to be in My storyline of history and to shape history. I have plans for nations that I am waiting to release through you. Agree with Me about what I say. Agree with who I say you are. Agree and decree. Align your mouth with My heart and truth and write a new decree that trumps what the enemy is doing. Speak your decrees. Watch and you will see! I have set you over nations and kingdoms and I touch your mouth with My power to overthrow and tear down what the enemy has done. And to build and plant My kingdom instead.

Ask Me to give you the nations as your inheritance, My Bride! The deliverance and harvest of nations is here and we are going forth together into the harvest fields that are ripe! I am receiving the full reward of My suffering!

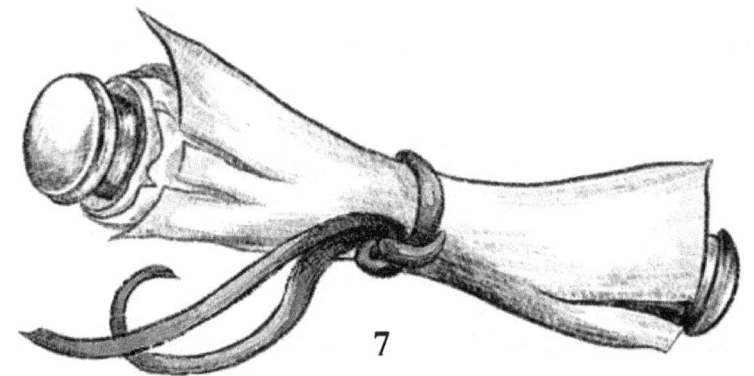

7

JUSTICE AT JUST THE RIGHT TIME

God mantled Mordecai, and Queen Esther, to accomplish His plan for an entire nation! God literally "infiltrated" the Persian government through them! Although the enemy has been systematically and diabolically infiltrating America (and many nations) in multitudes of ways, God has been infiltrating the enemy's camp with *His* people to bring forth *His* kingdom purposes! He is positioning His Mordecais, and Esthers in places of great influence. Much of this strategic positioning by the Lord is about the turnaround for the *nation*.

Sitting at the King's Gate

Can you imagine the challenges that Mordecai faced as an exile? But, Mordecai did not give up. Despite being a Jew in exile in a foreign land, he served the king with integrity and excellence. This is very much like Daniel and Joseph. Mordecai surely didn't agree with all that the king of Persia represented and believed, but nevertheless, he continued to selflessly serve him. He faithfully watched over the king at the gates of his palace, day and night.

Consider this: Mordecai was just as instrumental as Esther in preserving the nation. The Book of Esther says several times that he "sat at the king's gate". What a statement. *Gates, in ancient times, were foundational in a city.* They were the place of commerce, civic government and more. Gates clearly offer protection to the city and its people. The gates, along with the gatekeepers, decided what went in and what went out--what was kept in and what stayed out. The elders took their places at the gates, as did the judges.

45

Mordecai was positioned at the "king's gate", so he sat in a governmental seat of authority, given to him by the king. Part of this involved watching over the king. A watchman is one who sees beyond to protect, who sees danger coming from far off and knows precisely what to do with this intel. A watchman is given the crucial charge to sound the alarm.

Chuck Pierce prophesied in 2018 that we are in a new era of the watchman anointing. This is keenly demonstrated in America--and Israel--in this crucial hour. The word "shamar" is an apt description of this kind of watching: it means to "watch, keep, guard and protect". This even applies to the way that we "keep" covenant with God individually and watch over the covenant that America is in with God!

Mutual Honor: Double Trouble to the Enemy

The governmental seat that Mordecai held empowered him to overhear the plot of two of the king's doorkeepers, who became angry with the king and were plotting his assassination. Mordecai took his intel and shrewdly shared it with his cousin Esther. Esther, as queen, was in position to speak directly to the king about it. The plot was exposed and the evil men were killed. Curse reversed!

We see a mutual cooperation and honoring of each other in this exchange. Mordecai honored Esther and the position she held as queen, knowing her influence with the king. Queen Esther boldly told the king about the intel but she credited Mordecai, giving honor to him. This interweaving together foiled the assassination attempt and preserved the life of the king!

This is reminiscent of King David and how the Lord trained him in the wilderness as a shepherd. He killed a lion and a bear and that prepared him for the ultimate face-off with Goliath, the giant whom the entire army was deathly afraid of. His dramatic take-down of Goliath brought about the turnaround for the entire nation--but it started years earlier with the "small" victories over the lion and the bear. That wilderness season was also the appointed time in his life when David, alone on the hillsides with his sheep, developed a deep intimacy with God.

Similarly, Mordecai watched at the king's gate and successfully dealt with these two guards plotting evil. This not only spared the king's life, it prepared Mordecai to take on a much bigger contender, Haman. Mordecai and Esther's defeat of Haman, like David's defeat of Goliath, ultimately led to national preservation and a people awakening to the warrior within them.

How has the Lord been training you? What are the "lions and bears" in your life you have defeated--or may be facing? Remember, ultimately they can serve as spiritual "trainers" for you--building up your spiritual strength and fortitude and wisdom! As you partner with the Lord to take out the "lions and bears" in your life, He is equipping you and enlarging your spirit to deal with and defeat the "major league" threats that not only affect you and your family--but your city, state and even nation.

Night and Day

Not only did Mordecai diligently watch over the king, but his daughter-cousin Esther as well. The Word says that he went to the palace daily to check on her well-being (Esther 2:11). This is a word for us regarding what and whom God has called us to watch over--it may be a season, but it's not a part-time endeavor. *We need to be all-in. This is an hour where we are required to be alert and on the wall "night and day".*

This will take different forms in different seasons but the point is to be awake and ready to move at God's command--and to sound the alarm when and where it's necessary. Know your position and know whom you're positioned with. Be ready in season and out of season to release the Word of God and the prophetic word of God. Be ready to mobilize as His watchman (2 Timothy 4:2).

Mordecai reminded Esther of her foundation of faith in God and Jewish heritage--and her identity as a queen. He called out her courage and destiny as one whom God appointed to rescue a nation. He helped her with "knowing the times and the season and what she ought to do", like the sons of Issachar (1 Chronicles 12:32). The timing of God is key, especially when lives are at stake--and an entire people group!

Mordecai and Esther needed each other and God planned it that way! Their destinies were inextricably linked. This is why, especially in this time of history, it is important to know whom God has called you to align with--and when to align with them. The same is true for those whom God has *not* appointed you to be aligned with and to disconnect from those people when He directs you to do so. Often, this is about the distinction between "good and best" in your life.

How about you? Are you willing to watch over those whom God has appointed to you with renewed resolve? Are you willing to even watch over the leaders of your civic government, state and nation--even if you don't fully agree with them? Will you lay down your agenda and political persuasions in order to pray for the ones sitting in the seats of our government? This is a test of spiritual maturity and it's also a significant honor that God entrusts to governmental intercessors.

The term "governmental intercessor" ultimately refers to the government of God, the kingdom. Governmental intercession and worship flow from "heaven to earth". It's about bringing the kingdom of God to bear into the earth realm. As the ekklesia, we are ultimately not called to build a political party, we are called to build the kingdom of God.

Beware of the Political Spirit

We are in an unprecedented hour regarding the political climate of America. The very life of the nation is at stake--and in many ways, the nations. It's vital for us as believers to "come up higher" (Revelation 4:1) and realize that much of what we are seeing unfold is not earthly, it's spiritual. "For we do not wrestle against flesh and blood, but against principalities, against powers, against the rulers of the darkness of this age, against spiritual hosts of wickedness in the heavenly places" (Ephesians 6:12). This is a key Scripture to put at the forefront of our hearts and minds in these days.

If we forget this truth, we can fall prey to a multitude of traps by the enemy--especially pride and presumption. Fear and anger. Deception and manipulation. And the religious spirit and the political spirit. We must remember this is primarily a spiritual war--not a political one!

The political spirit has been around for ages. Apostle Faisal Malick teaches that it is a false governing spirit that is opposes the government of God and even destinies. It has a motive to kill and destroy, but it looks good while it's doing it.

It will ruthlessly make alliances with other spirits, like the religious spirit or the Jezebel spirit, to further its hidden agenda--whatever it takes. Ultimately, it's a "strongman" and a Herodian spirit. Mark 8:15 warns us of the "leaven of Herod". I encourage you to avail yourself to the profound revelation that Apostle Malick has on this subject in his book *The Political Spirit*. It's crucial truth for believers in this hour of history, especially for kingdom leaders.

No Compromise

In Esther 3:1-4 we see a clear picture of Mordecai's unwavering devotion to God and his integrity--two key character traits that are vital in this hour in which deep deception and compromise abound: "And all the king's servants who were within the king's gate bowed and paid homage to Haman, for so the king had commanded concerning him. But Mordecai would not bow or pay homage." Whether in public or private, the only one Mordecai would bow to and worship was Almighty God.

A few chapters later in the Book of Esther, we read an incredible turn of events: "That night the king could not sleep. So one was commanded to bring the book of the records of the chronicles; and they were read before the king. And it was found written that Mordecai had told of Bigthana and Teresh, two of the king's eunuchs, the doorkeepers who had sought to lay hands on King Ahasuerus. Then the king said, "What honor or dignity has been bestowed on Mordecai for this?" And the king's servants who attended him said, "Nothing has been done for him" (Esther 6:1-3). Essentially, Mordecai's exposure of the assassination plot had gone unrecognized. But, God saw it all. At the right time, the Lord brought this to the attention of the king--in a most remarkable way.

Directly after this providential discovery, listen to what unfolds in Esther 6:6-9 as the king speaks with Haman:

"What shall be done for the man whom the king delights to honor?"

"Now Haman thought in his heart, 'Whom would the king delight to honor more than me?' And Haman answered the king, 'For the man whom the king delights to honor, let a royal robe be brought which the king has worn, and a horse on which the king has ridden, which has a royal crest placed on its head. Then let this robe and horse be delivered to the hand of one of the king's most noble princes, that he may array the man whom the king delights to honor. Then parade him on horseback through the city square, and proclaim before him: 'Thus shall it be done to the man whom the king delights to honor!'"

"Then the king said to Haman, 'Hurry, take the robe and the horse, as you have suggested, and do so for Mordecai the Jew who sits within the king's gate! Leave nothing undone of all that you have spoken.'"

Justice at Just the Right Time

Isn't this amazing? *Just at the right time*, while having the chronicles of his reign read to him on a sleepless night, the king discovers what Mordecai did to spare his life. *Just at the right time*, Haman walks in and the king poses *just the right question*. Haman, in his pride, mistakenly thinks this is all about him so he asks big! He proposes the very best that the king has to be given to this "man the king delights to honor".

In a stunning turn of events, *just at the right time*, all of these items of honor end up being awarded to Haman's targeted enemy: Mordecai! This is justice! And this is "just at the right time justice"! Our God is sovereign!

Here's a word for you: what you have sown in obedience and honor to your King Jesus, you will reap at the right time. God sees you! He delights in all of your devotion to Him, especially in the "secret place" where no one else sees but Him. He sees your quiet acts of selflessness and "preferring others over yourself" in countless ways that no one else notices--out of your love for Him.

Just like Mordecai, at just the right time, there will be a promoting and an honoring for you. Keep serving and loving God with a pure heart, with wholehearted passion and uncompromising integrity. God has all the pieces on the chess board lined up. At just the right time, you will receive your reward. Don't grow weary in well doing because in due season you'll reap if you don't lost heart (Galatian 6:9). Your God-given reward, in this life and in heaven, will be far beyond what you can dream of--just like it was for Mordecai. "Just at the right time justice" is coming to you in ways that will leave you in holy shock and awe! And this is coming for America--and Israel--too!

From the Heart of Father God

I am calling you, child, as My Mordecai who will faithfully be alert, day and night, to "sit at the king's gate" as a governmental intercessor. I've extended a royal invitation to the intercessors of My heart and My power in this hour of America to sit at the king's gate. To watch over the government of America as My kingdom governmental intercessor.

Will you be a new gatekeeper of this hour who will not only watch and see in new ways, but also "watch the time" as the sons of Issachar did? As you seek Me and My ways, I give you living understanding of the time and season you are in and divine wisdom to know exactly what to do.

I mantle you as a Mordecai who will operate as a shamar watchman, seeking to keep and guard and protect that which is precious to Me. To even be a guardian of My covenant. To see and hear the enemy's plans before they are hatched like Elisha did, even assassination attempts like Mordecai overheard, and then bring the enemy to sound defeat. You are adorned with a glorious crown and a beautiful wreath, and you sit in a righteous seat of judgment as a judge in my government, mantled with my spirit of justice to turn every battle at the gates (Isaiah 28:5-6).

I am bringing justice at just the right time to you and your generational lines and your family. I am releasing justice to your nation and the nations! Stand and agree with Me and decree My purposes! My justice is manifesting in the end times harvest of the nations that is here!

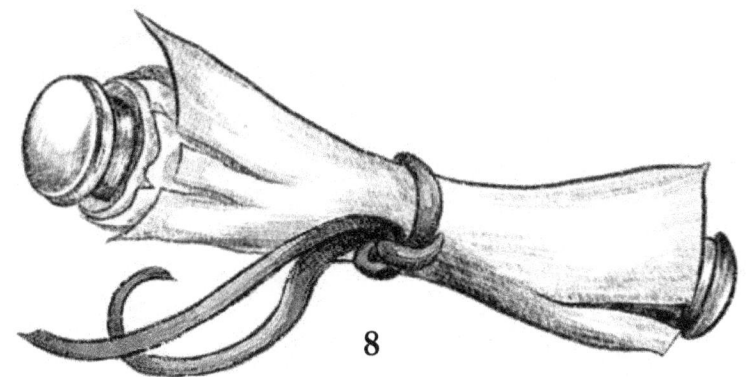

8

TRANSFIGURE AND RADIATE

The multi-faceted ways that God speaks are limitless. He even brings revelation through letters, numbers, dates and more! This is part of knowing "what time it is" like the sons of Issachar that we read about in the previous chapter. Mordecai and Esther knew what time it was prophetically-speaking--and they acted courageously and with wisdom in the timing of God. We are empowered by God to do this in our day as well!

Once again, a key Issachar time piece is the fact that we are in the Hebraic decade of the 80's, connected to the Hebrew letter "pey". This letter is the 17th letter of the Hebrew alphabet. The Lord highlighted several key 17s for this decade.

Hebraic Decade of 17: Matthew 17

The number 17 means "triumph" which means more than a victory, but domination over the enemy. It's a *complete* victory. Hear this over your life and nation for this decade: God is bringing triumph! At the head of the new Hebraic year 5780 (in September 2019), the Lord also showed me that *this decade (2020-2029) is a season of Matthew 17 and John 17.*

For several years, the Lord has been forming a prophetic word in me that His glory light within His sons and daughters, even as He calls us the "light of the world", is coming *out* of us in an unprecedented way! My spirit has been burning with the expectation that the *fullness of His glory within us will be seen in and through us in a way that we have not experienced before.* The Lord has related this to the Mount of Transfiguration account.

In Matthew 17, this account is dramatically revealed: "Six days later Jesus took Peter and the two brothers, Jacob [James] and John, and hiked up a high mountain to be alone. Then Jesus' appearance was dramatically altered. A radiant light as bright as the sun poured from his face. And his clothing became luminescent—dazzling like lightning. He was trans-figured before their very eyes. Then suddenly, Moses and Elijah appeared, and they spoke with Jesus" (Matthew 17:1-3 TPT).

Imagine yourself standing on the mountain and witnessing this sight: a "radiant light as bright as the sun" pouring from Jesus' face. Even His clothing was "dazzling like lighting". He was transfigured. Now ponder that this is *your* destiny, too! *To radiate and shine the light of Jesus Christ wherever you go as a "city on a hill"!*

Listen to this beautiful translation of Matthew 5:14-16 in the Passion Translation: "Your lives light up the world. Let others see your light from a distance, for how can you hide a city that stands on a hilltop? And who would light a lamp and then hide it in an obscure place? Instead, it's placed where everyone in the house can benefit from its light. So, don't hide your light! Let it shine brightly before others, so that the commendable things you do will shine as light upon them, and then they will give their praise to your Father in heaven." It's time for your light to shine so that all those who see you will encounter Father God and give Him praise!

The word for "transfigure" is the Greek word "metamorphoo" and it essentially means to be changed into a different form. Like the metamorphosis of a caterpillar to a butterfly. It's the same word used in 2 Corinthians 3:18: "But we all, with unveiled face, beholding as in a mirror the glory of the Lord, are being transformed into the same image from glory to glory, just as by the Spirit of the Lord." The word "transformed" in this Scripture is "metamorphoo", so we could say that we are being transfigured into the same image from glory to glory! Incredible.

The only other Scripture with "metamorphoo" (other than two verses in the Mount of Transfiguration account) is found in Romans 12:2: "And do not be conformed to this world, but be transformed by the renewing of your mind, that you may prove what is that good and acceptable and perfect will of God." *This is a profound revelation: we are transfigured, changed into a different form, by the renewing of our mind!* Ponder how powerful your thought life is as you encounter this Scripture with fresh eyes.

Hebraic Decade of 17: John 17

Another 17 that the Lord highlighted in connection to the 17th letter pey is John 17. One word that summarizes this chapter is: oneness. A strong word the Lord has given me for this decade is about our oneness with Father, Son and Holy Spirit. The Bride of Christ is stepping into a new dimension of this oneness with the Godhead and this is manifesting in a greater way in our spirit, soul and body--bringing renewed health and healing to us and through us.

I believe this oneness will also bring an entirely new dimension of healing and wholeness from trauma and the shattering that this can bring. Trauma is a like a generational pandemic that virtually every human being is negatively impacted by. It creates manifold problems and pain. The enemy, like Haman, has mistakenly believed for ages that trauma is his demonic ace up his sleeve. But just like God is bringing a turning of the tide! His manifold wisdom, love and power is being released in greater ways as the solution to this shattering of trauma. Remember: trauma to triumph!

Just like He did in Mordecai's life, God is bringing unprecedented restoration which means "better than it was before"! I also heard Him say that the decade of pey is the Decade of "Peyback"! It's "peyback" time. We are receiving astonishing payback, restitution and 7-fold justice for the harm and injustices the enemy has done to us and our bloodlines! Justice at just the right time is coming to us!

Oneness and Wholeness

Watch in this new era how God releases healing to us in dimensions that we have never seen before! Not only that, our oneness with Father, Son and Holy Spirit is also manifesting in fresh, innovative ways between us and among us as believers, according to the promises in John 17. This releases profound healing and wholeness--not just to individuals, but families, churches, cities and nations.

This oneness and unity among believers are about the *kingdom* of God and they are absolutely foundational to this end times harvest of souls, this Third Great Awakening. Pre-believers will see the love and unity that we have with Father, Son and Holy Spirit reflected in our love and unity with each other. They will take notice and seek out the God whom we know and love! These hungry hearts will recognize Him in us and in our relationships with each other and cry out for this authentic love! This is what each of us was made for.

Pause for a moment and carefully take in Jesus' prayer for you in John 17:19-24 (TPT):

"And I ask not only for these disciples,
but also for all those who will one day
believe in me through their message.
I pray for them all to be joined together as one
even as you and I, Father, are joined together as one.
I pray for them to become one with us

so that the world will recognize that you sent me.
For the very glory you have given to me I have given them
so that they will be joined together as one
and experience the same unity that we enjoy.
You live fully in me and now I live fully in them
so that they will experience perfect unity,
and the world will be convinced that you have sent me,
for they will see that you love each one of them
with the same passionate love that you have for me.
Father, I ask that you allow everyone that you have given to me
to be with me where I am!
Then they will see my full glory—
the very splendor you have placed upon me
because you have loved me even before the beginning of time."

Hebraic Decade of the 80's: Matthew 17 and John 17 Dovetailed

It's profound to consider how Matthew 17 and John 17 actually dovetail with each other. This convergence truly does release the 17 of triumph! This is clearly seen in John 17:1-5 (TPT) which has a reverberation of Matthew 17:

"This is what Jesus prayed as he looked up into heaven,
"Father, the time has come.
Unveil the glorious splendor of your Son
so that I will magnify your glory!
You have already given me authority
over all people so that I may give
the gift of eternal life to all those that you have given to me.
Eternal life means to know and experience you
as the only true God,
and to know and experience Jesus Christ,
as the Son whom you have sent.
I have glorified you on the earth
by faithfully doing everything you've told me to do.
So my Father, restore me back to the glory
that we shared together when we were face-to-face
before the universe was created."

Incredible! These are some of the final words of Jesus before He ascended back to heaven--adding even more weight to their meaning. He speaks of the time coming for the unveiling of His glorious splendor--to magnify His Father's glory! Can you hear the echo of Matthew 17 in this passage? Are you catching this for yourself, too? *The time of your "unveiling" is also appointed by God!* Through intense trials, Mordecai was unveiled and became even more of a respected leader among his people.

I don't know precisely what this unveiling will look like for the Bride of Christ as a whole. I do know that we have been in an intense preparation and purification season, like Esther and Mordecai, in order to shine in our unveiling--for the glory of our Father God!

Perhaps what is most gripping in this passage from John 17 is verse 5 in which Jesus speaks of being restored back to the glory that He shared with Father God when they were face-to-face, before the universe was created. This remarkable return to original intent is for you and me right now!

Our Father God is truly restoring us to that glory that we shared together even before the universe was created! Ponder this deeply--and let great hope arise!

Original Intent of Male and Female

In Mordecai and Esther, we see *another dimension of "original intent"--for male and female.* God brought together a complementary coalescing of what Mordecai carried as distinctly male and what Esther possessed as uniquely female. This is not about stereotypes; this is about the original design of our Creator God. It's obvious that the definition, the essence, of male and female is under severe attack by the enemy in this hour.

There is immense confusion he is trying to stir up--because he understands the power of original intent and is seeking to destroy it through deep deception. Therefore, it's even more important for us to be grounded in the truth and to know our Father God and His love, and therefore know who we are as male and female. It's imperative for us to flow in that unashamedly and to celebrate the differences as we partner together for God's purposes! Godly masculinity and femininity are something to rejoice in!

This fresh expression of original intent for male and female is foundational and a hallmark of this new apostolic era we have stepped into. For too long, men have largely been ridiculed and caricaturized by Western culture. Women have been objectified and subjugated--held back in many ways. The ungodly ideology of feminism has grossly undermined both sexes and shredded the fabric of marriage, family and morality in our society. But, the tide is turning and it's time for reformation!

It's time for a return to original intent so both men and women, male and female, can arise into the fullness of who God made us to be. As we fully depend on Father God by faith, there is a holy interdependence between male and female that flows--we need each other!

The Mordecais of this hour have a destiny that is intertwined in a heavenly way with the Esthers. As they move in what God has appointed for them from *before* the foundation of the world, they will see a multiplication of joy and fulfillment. Mordecais need Esthers and Esthers need Mordecais, and there is a humility that is required for this holy weaving together.

This unity and oneness are a pleasing, fragrant oil to God. This reminds me of the fragrant oil and perfumes that Esther, a picture of the prepared Bride, possessed. Psalm 133 beautifully illustrates this:

"Behold, how good and how pleasant it is
For brethren to dwell together in unity!
It is like the precious oil upon the head,
Running down on the beard,
The beard of Aaron,
Running down on the edge of his garments.
It is like the dew of Hermon,
Descending upon the mountains of Zion;
For there the Lord commanded the blessing—
Life forevermore."

As men and women flow in unity in Holy Spirit, His oil flows down upon our heads. And the Lord commands a blessing of *life*. When we as men and women move in synch with who God called us to be in a kingdom way, we will rise up together. This partnership is what God had in mind from the beginning and honor is a key part of this. As fiery prophetic worship leader James Nesbit declares, "Honor unlocks glory".

This holy partnership will bring about an entirely new dimension of building the kingdom of God. Watch what God does to not only bring restoration in this dimension but radical reformation. Reformation is about change, ultimately a transformation of *societies*.

Watch how this impacts marriages and families, the building blocks of society! These kingdom embassies are precisely what are foundational for building, and sustaining, this Third Great Awakening!

Generations Braided Together

Another component that Mordecai, along with Esther, possessed is unity between the generations. It's not clear how much older Mordecai was than Esther, but we can see that he cared for her as a father. This speaks of two generations intertwining. This is another key component in this hour of awakening in our nation. *The generations are coming together in a greater way--we need to unite if we desire the fullness of what God has for us.* This uniting is also a return to original intent.

Each generation carries a unique sound in the orchestra of God and each individual carries a specific note. Just as an orchestra must have each musician and instrument for the full sound, so it is with the generations. God is tuning each of us to His heart, His frequency, so that He can play us like His holy instruments of righteousness to release this new sound for this new era!

There is a transfiguration, oneness and unity coming to the ekklesia in America in this hour that is unprecedented and utterly necessary for this new move of God that is here. God is taking what the enemy meant for evil to draw us closer together!

Another major expression is the full circle of original intent for "Jew and gentile" coming together as "one new man" (Ephesians 2:14-16). This has been happening in notable ways particularly in the past several decades. Volumes have been written about the "one new man", but in brief, this is a profoundly central piece of what God is doing in this hour of history.

From the Heart of Father God

My child, I bless your oneness with Me. I am your Father God and you are the Bride of My Son and My Holy Spirit dwells within you. I call forth a deepening of intimacy with each of Us in the Godhead--in Our oneness you will experience a greater oneness with Us and this will manifest in your spirit, soul and body. I am releasing greater healing and deliverance and wholeness, even from the shattering from trauma and its effects, from this oneness.

As you experience this deeper oneness, this is manifesting in your relationships with other believers according to my Son's prayer in John 17. I am restoring you to the glory that you shared with Me face-to-face even before I created the universe! This is causing the doxa, My glory light within you, to shine brighter and brighter! This truly is a time of your transfiguration, just like My Son experienced on the mountain. Shine brightly for Me and the world will see!

I'm raising up the Mordecais right alongside the Esthers. For you cannot do what I've called you to do alone--there is a holy interdependence. There is a fresh apostolic anointing for the true male and female to come forth and to honor one another and who I have made you to be. There is a fresh prophetic anointing to be My mouthpiece and timepiece for the deliverance and destiny of a nation. This is a manifestation of the original intent for the foundation of the ekklesia, the foundation of the apostle and the prophet, that I am bringing forth in this new era of history.

I'm calling you forth to align with the generations. Regardless of your age, you have a destiny to fulfill and it is connected to those "ahead" and "behind" you, so be intentional about partnering with them and walk in humility and love. No one is too young and no one is too old. Everyone has a part to play and a note to sound! This alignment is connected to the "synergy of the ages"! The great cloud of witnesses is a part of this interweaving! You all move AS ONE in Me!

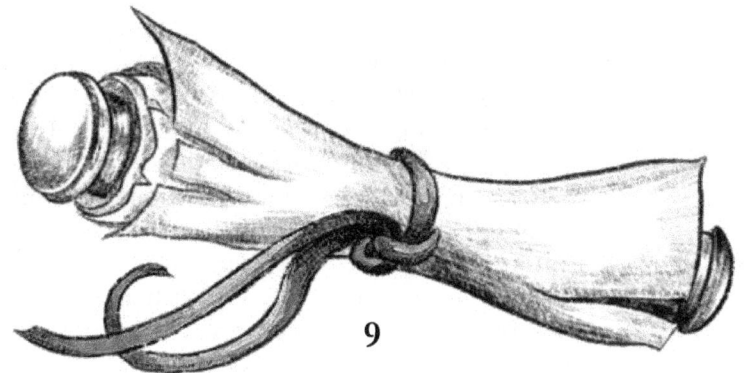

9

TURNING OF THE TABLES

Marvel afresh at more details of how God brought a stunning turn of events to an entire nation. As we learned earlier, in the moment of utter peril, Esther was moved by the Spirit of God to call a corporate fast. One of the central dimensions of fasting is a "setting aside for a drawing near".

Fasting allows for a greater "First love focus" on the Lord as roadblocks to intimacy with Him are revealed and removed. One fruit of fasting is often key revelation that comes from the renewed closeness with the Lord.

After this three-day fast the entire nation entered into, Esther received a strategy from heaven: host two banquets. In Esther 7, the king and Haman are dining with Esther--at the second banquet. The king asks her, again, "What is your petition, Queen Esther? It shall be granted you. And what is your request, up to half the kingdom? It shall be done!" (v. 1).

Once again, we see the hand of God upon this queen to receive such favor from the king. We also see this favor upon Mordecai's life.

Turning of the Tables

Esther, knowing intuitively that this is her moment to make the big "ask", opens up her mouth and brings this bold request--and reveals her identity: "If I have found favor in your sight, O king, and if it pleases the king, let my life be given me at my petition, and my people at my request. For we have been sold, my people and I, to be destroyed, to be killed, and to be annihilated. Had we been sold as male and female slaves, I would have held my tongue, although the enemy could never compensate for the king's loss" (vv. 3-4).

Outraged, King Ahasuerus said to Queen Esther, "Who is he, and where is he, who would dare presume in his heart to do such a thing?" In response, Esther brings the hammer down, "The adversary and enemy *is* this wicked Haman!" (v. 6). The next part of this verse is truly stunning: "So Haman was terrified before the king and queen" (v. 6b).

This is where we are at in America. The enemy has been ruthlessly terrorizing in many dimensions, even like that ancient Amalekite spirit that terrorized the Israelites, but *now* the tables are turning. We are a bold people rising up with the roar of the Lion of the Tribe of Judah and *we are the ones who are now terrorizing the enemy!* Let your high praise to Yahweh arise and send terror into the enemy's camp!

Esther chapter 7 ends with this sequence: the king is enraged, a wise idea comes from a eunuch to use the gallows that Haman made for Mordecai to instead be the means of Haman's death, and then God's final word on the matter is revealed. In verse 10 we see an extraordinary turning of tables: "So they hanged Haman on the gallows that he had prepared for Mordecai." Selah.

Victory and the Spoils of the Enemy

This stunning account continues in chapter 8: "On that day King Ahasuerus gave Queen Esther the house of Haman, the enemy of the Jews. And Mordecai came before the king, for Esther had told how he *was related* to her. So, the king took off his signet ring, which he had taken from Haman, and gave it to Mordecai; and Esther appointed Mordecai over the house of Haman" (v.1-2). Remarkable.

Mordecai is given the very ring, symbolizing the king's authority, that was on his archenemy's hand. Mordecai also appointed over Haman's house, his estate. This is incredible redemption.

Esther could have stopped at that point. Her life was spared and Mordecai was promoted. But, she wasn't content with just herself and Mordecai being delivered. She pressed in bravely and continued her quest for deliverance--for her people.

She boldly, but humbly, made another appeal to the king, knowing that the original decree he authorized (written by Haman) still stood legally. The Jewish people were still facing extinction.

"And the king held out the golden scepter toward Esther. So Esther arose and stood before the king, and said, 'If it pleases the king, and if I have found favor in his sight and the thing seems right to the king and I am pleasing in his eyes, let it be written to revoke the letters devised by Haman, the son of

Hammedatha the Agagite, which he wrote to annihilate the Jews who *are* in all the king's provinces. For how can I endure to see the evil that will come to my people? Or how can I endure to see the destruction of my countrymen?'" (Esther 8:4-6). Hear her heart's cry in this statement: "How can I endure to see the destruction of my countrymen?"

New Decree

Several verses later, we read about the "new decree" which Esther and Mordecai were empowered to write--even with the king's signet ring. Note that they did this together. This ring is no ordinary ring of the king. Once again, it symbolizes the very authority of the king which "no one can revoke". The decree was written and the king's scribes went to work.

Couriers on fast horses were sent to swiftly deliver the new decree out to each province where the Jewish people lived. Can you imagine the amazement and radical joy on the faces of the Jewish people when the read this new decree, overriding their death sentence, in their hometown being posted? Suddenly! Miraculous deliverance!

"By these letters the king permitted the Jews who were in every city to gather together and protect their lives—to destroy, kill, and annihilate all the forces of any people or province that would assault them, both little children and women, and to plunder their possessions, on one day in all the provinces of King Ahasuerus, on the thirteenth day of the twelfth month, which is the month of Adar" (Esther 8:11-12).

As we read in a previous chapter, the Jewish people had to rise up and defend themselves and their families--they had to war though they had not dealt with war for several generations! But God supernaturally empowered them for triumph over their enemies!

In pondering these "letters of life", it's remarkable to consider that the Apostle Paul speaks of us, in the New Covenant, as "living letters". We are like a living decree of the Lord, releasing His Word, power and love. "As a result of our ministry, you are living letters written by Christ, not with ink but by the Spirit of the living God—not carved onto stone tablets but on the tablets of tender hearts" (2 Corinthians 3:3 TPT).

Great Light, Gladness, Joy and Honor

Listen to the astonishing conclusion of this drama in Esther 8: "So Mordecai went out from the presence of the king in royal apparel of blue and white, with a great crown of gold and a garment of fine linen and purple; and the city of Shushan rejoiced and was glad. The Jews had light and gladness, joy and honor. And in every province and city, wherever the king's command

and decree came, the Jews had joy and gladness, a feast and a holiday. Then many of the people of the land became Jews, because fear of the Jews fell upon them" (vv.15-17).

The Jews had "light"--the light of God penetrating the utter darkness they had been in. Instead of a death sentence and despair, they possessed gladness, joy and honor. They celebrated a feast and even made it a holiday. Could there be any more of a dramatic turn of events? Only God could do this!

How profound that this turn of events also led to the holy awe and reverence of God falling upon those who did not know the God of the Jewish people--prompting them to worship Him! In this passage we see multiple dimensions of "turning of tables" for God's appointed victory--and even beyond victory to triumph! Even those who weren't Jewish benefitted greatly!

This underscores the truth that *our personal breakthrough or corporate breakthrough is often connected to much greater breakthroughs than we can often imagine.* May God give us greater vision and bigger dreams as we partner with Him to see His dreams fulfilled in this hour of history!

One of the most captivating verses in the Book of Esther is found in chapter 9:1: "Now in the twelfth month, that is, the month of Adar, on the thirteenth day, the time came for the king's command and his decree to be executed. On the day that the enemies of the Jews had hoped to overpower them, the opposite occurred, in that the Jews themselves overpowered those who hated them." Hear this for yourself and your circumstances--for America and Israel, two covenant nations who are in covenant with each other.

The enemy has been working overtime to harass, oppress and divide the ekklesia in this hour, to confine and inflict great harm and fear. He has been rapidly accelerating antichrist agendas globally. He has been seeking to overpower us and intimidate us—even take us out. But, *now* the tables are turning.

A shift is happening and we are fully awakening to who God is and who we are in Him--and the delegated and earned authority we possess. *We are now overpowering the enemy!* The harvest is coming in! We are the enemy's worst nightmare--and God's end times champions arising in triumph!

Purim: Appointed Time of Joy

The second half of Esther 9 speaks of Mordecai and Esther writing another letter, regarding the feast of Purim: "So they called these days Purim, after the name Pur. Therefore, because of all the words of this letter, what they had seen concerning this matter, and what had happened to them, the Jews established and imposed it upon themselves and their descendants and all who would join them, that without fail they should celebrate these two days every year, according to the written instructions and according to the prescribed time, that these days should be remembered and kept throughout every generation, every family, every province, and every city, that these days of Purim should not fail to be observed among the Jews, and that the memory of them should not perish among their descendants" (vv.26-28).

Ponder the comprehensive and lasting nature of these instructions: for every family, province, city and generations to observe the days of Purim-- that the memory of them should not perish among their descendants. To this day, Jewish people celebrate Purim and it's our joy as believers in Yeshua to do the same. *It's a glorious time to celebrate our God of the impossible and to trust Him to do even more impossible turning of tables--even through us!* It's a time to watch God miraculously bring the spoils of the enemy to us as His people!

In this passage of Esther 9:26-28, you can hear the echo of "Never forget" which is also the cry of many Jewish (and Gentile) people today regarding the Holocaust. This genocide was diabolically engineered by a man operating in a Haman spirit--Hitler--in which 6 million-plus Jews were annihilated. Shockingly, some people today are actually coming into agreement with a spirit of deception that denies the Holocaust took place!

May we be "on the wall" in prayer as watchmen (Isaiah 62:6-7), stand up against antisemitism and take bold action like Mordecai and Esther did in their day, to declare "Never forget!" This is very central to Father God's heart. Israel and the Jewish people will always be "the apple of His eye" (Zechariah 2:8).

Greatness and Light Increasing

The Book of Esther ends with shining accolades about Mordecai. "And King Ahasuerus imposed tribute on the land and on the islands of the sea. Now all the acts of his power and his might, and the account of the greatness of Mordecai, to which the king advanced him, are they not written in the book of the chronicles of the kings of Media and Persia?" (vv. 1-2). In the end, Mordecai became "greater and greater" because "he was well received by the multitude of his brethren, seeking the good of his people and speaking peace to all his countrymen" (v. 3).

This is a word for you. *You are called to selflessly seek the good of your people, not just your own good, and release peace to your family, community and nation as a peacemaker.* This is who you are as a son or daughter of God. Apart from Him you can do nothing, but with Him you can do all things.

His greatness is on the inside of you. His greatness was meant to be displayed in "greater and greater" ways. God's "doxa", which is His manifest presence and glory, dwells within us and one of the meanings of doxa is "ever increasing" and "brilliance".

The glory light of God and His government, His kingdom, within you is ever increasing (Isaiah 9:7) and radiating! We are light bearers of this hour! Watch how God will decimate and destroy the enemy's kingdom simply through the sound and light that He has placed within you! Truly, now is the time for you to arise and shine in the glory of the Lord (Isaiah 60:1-2).

Full Circle: Mordecai Mantle

In this final chapter, I will end as I began with *The Mordecai Mantle*. A full circle. The word "Gilgal", the place where Joshua required his men to come into covenant with God through circumcision before crossing over into the Promised Land, means "full circle". It also means "rolling away of the stone, rolling away of reproach".

God is speaking to the Bride of Christ in America through the Gilgal account: our spiritual hearts are being circumcised afresh, the flesh is coming off our hearts and we are renewing our covenant with Him, both personally and nationally. *God is also rolling away the reproach of "Egypt" and "Egyptian captivity" off of His Bride and America in this hour.* We are coming out of Babylon (Jeremiah 51), which again is a word that God gave me in 2017.

How remarkable that after 400 years in slavery in Egypt, God's people were miraculously delivered and set free—and America crossed that same threshold in celebrating her 400th anniversary of her covenant with God on November 11, 2020! This is a profound prophetic marker in the history of the United States that also holds great prophetic significance for our future.

November 11, 1620 is when the Mayflower Compact was signed by our forefathers to establish this nation for the glory of God and the advancement of the Christian faith. A freedom nation--for His glory! By covenant!

Purim Full Circle

In connection to Purim, there is a tradition to read the Book of Esther twice during this holiday. It's called the Megillah, which means "scroll". The Scroll of Esther is read, and it is distinctively the only one out of five such scrolls to be read from a handwritten parchment scroll.

What's remarkable is that Megillah comes from the root word "galal" which is also a root word for Gilgal! Once again, it means "full circle; rolling away of the stone; rolling away of reproach and wheel". Purim is historically a time of full circles for the Jewish people and there is a profound, miraculous FULL CIRCLE that is now in motion.

I sound the trumpet again that the time is *now* for the Mordecais in this hour of history to find fresh courage in their relationship with God and make a decision to boldly arise in faith. The righteous are as bold as a lion

(Proverbs 28:1). It's also time for the Mordecais to champion the Esthers in their lives and ascend together--for God's call to bring deliverance in every sphere He has appointed to them.

The Book of Esther is the account of one of the most astonishing turnarounds in history and right now, as we have seen, there are similar circumstances we are facing in America--and many nations. The core turnaround is a genuine turning of our hearts back to the Lord in repentance--and by the grace of God this is happening. His kindness is leading us to teshuvah.

Ultimately, these appointed turnarounds are setting the stage for this last great move of the Spirit of God on the earth and the global harvest of souls that is upon us! It's already here! But, once again, this Third Great Awakening is gaining in momentum in ways we have never seen before.

Where has God appointed you in this end times harvest field? What gate are you called to watch at? Who is the Esther(s) that you are called to come alongside? How has God equipped you to build His kingdom? What are the decrees you are called to write and speak?

Remember, God has appointments for you and ways to partner with Him and align with others that can literally shift your family, city—and nation! He has been preparing you "for such a time as this" to arise fearlessly and play your part in the justice and deliverance that God wants to release. For His glory!

Stand up and receive your Mordecai mantle from the Lord in His appointed time and align with the Esthers that He sovereignly places on your path. Work for the welfare and well-being of the people you are called to and the nation God has planted you in. Spend yourself on a cause much greater than you--the Third Great Awakening and the harvest of souls that is here!

Even in the midst of unprecedented chaos, deception and spiritual warfare in the nations, the turning of the tables is happening. The kingdoms of this world are becoming the kingdom of our God (Revelation 11:15). Your time is now and you have been anointed and appointed by God to build His kingdom and radiate His glory!

Arise, Mordecai!

From the Heart of Father God

My child, it's good to remember and to never forget. Never forget what I have done for you, out of My great love for you, in giving you My only Son to die in your place. You are justified, forgiven, cleansed, healed, delivered and saved by His shed blood on the cross. May the joy of your salvation be restored in every way. Never forget what I have done in history to preserve My chosen people, the Jewish people, because this was ultimately for your salvation. Pray for My chosen people and for the peace of Jerusalem, for Israel, in this hour. Your prayers are needed and your prayers can shift what is happening in the Middle East and the nations.

Just as I mantled Mordecai to work for the good of his people and speak for the peace of his countrymen, so I have mantled you to, from your oneness with Me, to work for the good of your own people, your nation. You are not only a spokesman of My shalom, you are a carrier of it. Diffuse my peace like a fragrance wherever you go. Build altars of worship to Me, the God of Peace, like Gideon did through a lifestyle of worshipping Me.

Remember that there is a turning of the tables coming that will astound you. The day is coming closer. Though many nations are hanging in the balance, the Haman spirit is hanging on its own gallows. This will release you into a time of great light, gladness and joy. More joy than your heart can even hold when you watch what I will do miraculously. Promotions will come and spoils from the battle. Some of your greatest places of battle will be your greatest places of victory.

Trust me, My child. Great triumph awaits.

ACKNOWLEDGEMENTS

Jason, Hannah, Haley and Moses
You are the light of my life! You are my joy and my crown! You are my greatest gifts in this world. Each of you is an answer to some of the deepest prayers I have prayed. I love and treasure each of you more than you can fathom. I could literally write books, and in some ways I have, regarding the rich destiny that is upon each of your lives. And, I'm honored to be an integral part of each of your tremendous storylines. I'm proud of who each of you is and who you are becoming.

We have many prophetic words about having a family enterprise that is radically creative, communicating the gospel of the kingdom in new ways. This is coming to pass! We are a family of kingdom pioneers--and explorers. My heart is burning as I ponder what's next for our family. We are going to new heights together in the love of Father God—and releasing His love and power in this Third Great Awakening. We are of those who are "turning the world upside down" or should I say "right side up"--back to its God-given original intent. The best is truly yet to come for us!

Dave and Julie Carlson
You are a beloved son and daughter of Abba and a lover of the presence of God. You live for and from God's manifest presence as a lifestyle, and steward it with such humility, honor and love--at Josiah Center and beyond. Your hearts have been refined in the fire and both of you have one of the purest hearts I've encountered. You are exceptional kingdom forerunners of

reformation who are leading the way in this Awakening and move of God we are in.

Your apostolic mantle and authority are immense and ever-increasing—deeply influencing a city, state, nation and the nations. You are a true spiritual father and mother. I am thrilled to watch the Lord take you, and your message, to heights and places you cannot even imagine—for His glory. You are "boldly going where no man has gone before", like King David did in his hour of history, in many dimensions to "pull the future into the now" and build the kingdom of God.

Thank you for the many ways you joyfully, but sacrificially, call out the gold and champion others, including myself, so that we can soar our destinies for the glory of God. You are dear to me and my family. It is an absolute joy and honor to partner with you as "burning ones" to see this end times move of God fully catalyzed, and a billion+ harvest of souls brought in! All for the glory of the King of Glory!

Jon and Jolene Hamill
You are dear friends and remarkable shamar governmental prophets to America and the nations. Not only do signs and wonders follow you, the two of you truly are a sign and wonder. That's why "You can't make this stuff up" is a chorus in the song of your lives. It's also beautiful how you move together synergistically as prophets--as a couple--and model this to others.

You truly are the keepers of the covenant for America. Who can fathom such a high calling and the sacrifices you have made, and continue to make, to walk in this calling? You move in great power and governmental authority and remarkable prophetic accuracy—and you walk in humility, transparency, integrity and love. Sounds like "Christ in you, the hope of glory." You are honorable leaders who live a life of honoring God and others—and you are fun to be around! Mostly, your immense anointing is founded and nourished in a deep, genuine relationship with the Lord, and the resulting obedience, that clearly has marked both of you—for many years.

It is one of the highest honors and joys of my life to be a part of your Gideon group--to pray and intercede AS ONE for our great nation and for this remarkable calling on your lives. God is bringing one of the most stunning turnarounds in history to the United States through this massive harvest coming in. Your forerunning as governmental prophets and intercessors has truly been one of the keys in this turning and Third Great Awakening that you are heralding. You are indeed spiritual Paul Reveres in this midnight hour of American history! Glory to God! Keep riding forth in triumph and joy!

Jon, thank you for the word that you released to me on my birthday about writing a book! That word is what set this book into motion.

Brian Hume

I stand amazed at how the Lord sovereignly intersected our paths through a 444 swirl! And the swirls and divine kingdom connections continue with frequency and fervor on this journey with Him! I am filled with anticipation for what is next.

You are a prophet who deeply carries the Father's heart—and has astonishing accuracy and detail in your words. This clearly comes from the "secret history with God", as you say, that has been cultivated with Him over decades. What defines you most is: beloved son of God. This is your identity and message that you live with great integrity and humility and purity. The heart of Father God flows so powerfully from you.

You also have an incredible apostolic anointing on your life that is continually connecting and gathering people, and helping them fully ascend into their destinies—and as one of them, I am grateful!

Your prophetic word to me, after reading a posting I did about Esther and Mordecai in 2019, is the other prophetic word that helped spark this book. Thank you for releasing that word from the Lord to me and your help in my editing of this book!

THE MORDECAI MANTLE

ABOUT THE AUTHOR

Lori Perz and her husband Jason, along with their three bright and shining children, are kingdom revolutionaries and reformers with a creative edge and vision for harvest. Lori has a fiery love for Yeshua and is a prophetic trumpet and scribe with an Issachar mantle in the ekklesia. She has a heart for Israel and the Jewish people and a passion for the Hebraic roots of the Christian faith. She is the Director of Prophetic Ministries at Josiah Center, a forerunning worship and apostolic center in St. Paul, MN centered on the Presence of God. Lori is also joyfully honored to be a part of the Gideon Group, a special ops intercessory team for Prophets Jon and Jolene Hamill of Lamplighter ministries.

Contact Lori at: ariseandshine444@protonmail.com.

www.ingramcontent.com/pod-product-compliance
Lightning Source LLC
Chambersburg PA
CBHW022124040426
42450CB00006B/831